Circulating Reference

Take the reference book you need home tonight and use it. Nifty right? As with all good things, there are a couple of catches. First, **no renewals**-someone else probably needs this book too. Second, **no holds**. Enjoy the new Circulating Reference!

U·X·L
American Decades
1920 · 1929

Tom Pendergast
& Sara Pendergast,
Editors

U·X·L®

THOMSON
★
GALE™

Detroit • New York • San Diego • San Francisco • Cleveland • New Haven, Conn. • Waterville, Maine • London • Munich

U•X•L American Decades, 1920–1929

Tom Pendergast and Sara Pendergast, Editors

Project Editors
Diane Sawinski, Julie L. Carnagie, and Christine Slovey

Editorial
Elizabeth Anderson

Permissions
Shalice Shah-Caldwell

Imaging and Multimedia
Dean Dauphinais

Product Design
Pamela A.E. Galbreath

Composition
Evi Seoud

Manufacturing
Rita Wimberley

For permission to use material from this product, submit your request via Web at http://www.gale-edit.com/permissions, or you may download our Permissions Request form and submit your request by fax or mail to:

Permissions Department
The Gale Group, Inc.
27500 Drake Rd.
Farmington Hills, MI 48331-3535
Permissions Hotline:
248-699-8006 or 800-877-4253, ext. 8006
Fax: 248-699-8074 or 800-762-4058

Cover photograph reproduced by permission of the Corbis Corporation.

While every effort has been made to ensure the reliability of the information presented in this publication, The Gale Group, Inc. does not guarantee the accuracy of the data contained herein. The Gale Group, Inc. accepts no payment for listing; and inclusion in the publication of any organization, agency, institution, publication, service, or individual does not imply endorsement of the editors or publisher. Errors brought to the attention of the publisher and verified to the satisfaction of the publisher will be corrected in future editions.

Vol. 1: 0-7876-6455-3
Vol. 2: 0-7876-6456-1
Vol. 3: 0-7876-6457-X
Vol. 4: 0-7876-6458-8
Vol. 5: 0-7876-6459-6
Vol. 6: 0-7876-6460-X
Vol. 7: 0-7876-6461-8
Vol. 8: 0-7876-6462-6
Vol. 9: 0-7876-6463-4
Vol. 10: 0-7876-6464-2

LIBRARY OF CONGRESS CATALOGING-IN-PUBLICATION DATA

U•X•L American decades
   p. cm.
Includes bibliographical references and index.
   Contents: v. 1. 1900-1910—v. 2. 1910-1919—v. 3.1920-1929—v. 4. 1930-1939—v. 5. 1940-1949—v. 6. 1950-1959—v. 7. 1960-1969—v. 8. 1970-1979—v. 9.1980-1989—v. 10. 1990-1999.
   Summary: A ten-volume overview of the twentieth century which explores such topics as the arts, economy, education, government, politics, fashions, health, science, technology, and sports which characterize each decade.
   ISBN 0-7876-6454-5 (set: hardcover: alk. paper)
   1. United States—Civilization—20th century—Juvenile literature. 2. United States—History—20th century—Juvenile literature. [1. United States—Civilization—20th century. 2. United States—History—20th century.] I. UXL (Firm) II. Title: UXL American decades. III. Title: American decades.
E169.1.U88 2003
973.91—dc21
2002010176

Printed in the United States of America
10 9 8 7 6 5 4 3

Contents

chapter six **Medicine and Health** **107**

Reader's Guide

U•X•L American Decades provides a broad overview of the major events and people that helped to shape American society throughout the twentieth century. Each volume in this ten-volume set chronicles a single decade and begins with an introduction to that decade and a timeline of major events in twentieth-century America. Following are eight chapters devoted to these categories of American endeavor:

• Arts and Entertainment

• Business and the Economy

• Education

• Government, Politics, and Law

• Lifestyles and Social Trends

• Medicine and Health

• Science and Technology

• Sports

These chapters are then divided into five sections:

Chronology: A timeline of significant events within the chapter's particular field.

Overview: A summary of the events and people detailed in that chapter.

Headline Makers: Short biographical accounts of key people and their achievements during the decade.

❖ **Topics in the News:** A series of short topical essays describing events and people within the chapter's theme.

✛ **For More Information:** A section that lists books and Web sites directing the student to further information about the events and people covered in the chapter.

OTHER FEATURES

Each volume of *U•X•L American Decades* contains more than eighty black-and-white photographs and illustrations that bring the events and people discussed to life and sidebar boxes that expand on items of high interest to readers. Concluding each volume is a general bibliography of books and Web sites that explore the particular decade in general and a thorough subject index that allows readers to easily locate the events, people, and places discussed throughout that volume of *U•X•L American Decades*.

COMMENTS AND SUGGESTIONS

We welcome your comments on *U•X•L American Decades* and suggestions for other history topics to consider. Please write: Editors, *U•X•L American Decades*, U•X•L, 27500 Drake Rd., Farmington Hills, MI 48331-3535; call toll-free: 1-800-877-4253; fax: 248-699-8097; or send e-mail via http://www.galegroup.com.

Chronology of the 1920s

1920:   Ex-U.S. Army officer John Thompson patents his machine gun, later nicknamed the "tommy gun."

1920:   The Menninger Clinic, which specializes in treating individuals with mental health afflictions, opens in Topeka, Kansas.

1920:   F. Scott Fitzgerald publishes his first novel, *This Side of Paradise*.

1920:   The Julliard Foundation is established in New York to encourage music in the United States.

1920:   **February 13** The Negro National League is organized in Kansas City, Missouri.

1920:   **August 20** The formation of what would become the National Football League (NFL) is set in motion when representatives from several Ohio-based professional football teams meet in Canton, Ohio.

1921:   **May** Construction begins on the Wrigley Building in Chicago. It will have a 32-story tower and 442,000 square feet of office space.

1922:   **May 5** Gabrielle "Coco" Chanel introduces Chanel No. 5, which will become the world's most famous perfume.

1922:   **May 30** The Lincoln Memorial, sculpted by Chester French, is dedicated in Washington, D.C.

1923:   George Eastman produces 16mm film for use by the general public, beginning the era of home movies.

1923: The first birth control clinic opens in New York City under the direction of Margaret Sanger.

1923: Zenith Radio is founded in Chicago, Illinois.

1923: **April 18** Yankee Stadium opens in New York. The New York Yankees will win their first world championship latter that year.

1924: **January 25–February 4** The first Winter Olympic Games are held in Chamonix, France.

1924: **March 10** J. Edgar Hoover is appointed acting director of the Federal Bureau of Investigation (FBI).

1924: **June** Chrysler Corporation is founded; the automaker's new car sells for approximately $1,500.

1924: **June 15** President Calvin Coolidge signs legislation granting U.S. citizenship to all Native Americans.

1925: Electrical engineer Vladimir Zworykin applies for a patent for color television.

1925: **June 1** The Yankees' Lou Gehrig plays the first of his record 2,130 consecutive games.

1925: **July 10** John T. Scopes goes on trial for teaching the theory of evolution to his students in Dayton, Tennessee.

1926: The National Broadcasting Company (NBC) forms a "network" by linking twenty-four radio stations.

1926: Sears Roebuck distributes fifteen million catalogs and twenty-three million special announcements per year to its customers.

1926: Greyhound Corporation begins bus service on American roads. General Motors is its major stockholder.

1926: Ernest Hemingway's first novel *The Sun Also Rises* is published.

1926: Langston Hughes publishes his first volume of poetry, *The Weary Blues*.

1926: **August 6** Gertrude Ederle becomes the first woman to swim the English Channel.

1927: Chrysler introduces the Plymouth car line, and soon afterward the new division introduces the mid-priced DeSoto sedan.

1927: Grauman's Chinese Theater, a legendary American movie palace, opens in Hollywood. The architectural theme is Oriental.

1927: **May 27** Aviator Charles A. Lindbergh arrives in Paris, France, after his 33½ hour solo flight across the Atlantic Ocean. This feat earns more attention than almost any other event of the decade.

1927: **September 30** Babe Ruth hits his sixtieth home run, breaking the record he set in 1921.

1927: **October** *The Jazz Singer,* the first feature-length motion picture with sequences that include singing and dialogue, premieres.

1927: **November** The Model A automobile is introduced by the Ford Motor Company.

1927: **November 21** The U.S. Supreme Court upholds the right of the state of Mississippi to place all nonwhite students in "colored" public schools.

1928: Minnesota Mining and Manufacturing (3M) Company markets cellophane tape as Scotch tape.

1928: **April 15** The New York Rangers become the first American hockey team to win the Stanley Cup championship.

1928: **September 3** Ty Cobb pinch-hits a double in a game against the Washington Senators. It is the last of his 4,189 major league hits.

1929: **February 23** The Brotherhood of Sleeping Car Porters, headed by A. Philip Randolph, is the first African American union to be chartered by the American Federation of Labor (AFL).

1929: **July 7** Transcontinental Air Transport announces a plan to offer coast-to-coast air and rail service, using airplanes over flatlands and railroad cars in the mountains.

1929: **September 11** The Fokker F32, the world's largest passenger plane, is unveiled.

1929: **October 29** The Dow Jones Industrial Average falls 30.57 points as the stock market crashes; $30 billion in market value evaporates on what comes to be known as "Black Tuesday."

The 1920s: An Overview

Unparalleled progress, creativity, adventure, and excitement characterized the United States during the 1920s. World War I (1914–18) had ended, and the Jazz Age began. The economy was booming. The stock market was soaring. The country was becoming a leader in international trade and banking. The increased need for jobs and services created new employment opportunities. The automobile industry in particular grew more powerful and sophisticated, and cars became fixtures in everyday American life. Middle-class and, to an extent, working-class families purchased them, and the Ford Motor Company's classic Model T remained the most popular and affordable car.

The metal and chemical industries made smooth transitions from war-oriented to consumer production. The building industry flourished in cities and suburbs across the land, and sleek urban skyscrapers and high-rise luxury apartments were constructed. Commercial airline flights began connecting America's cities. More young people were attending colleges and universities. Women were granted the right to vote and had more opportunities in the workplace. Americans generally were more fashion-conscious. Clothing became more daring, as women's hemlines rose from ankle to knee-length. Religion was less the centerpiece of American life. Instead of attending church, many people spent their weekends riding in their shiny new automobiles or watching the latest movies. The Volstead Act of 1920 had made intoxicating liquors illegal, but speakeasies opened around the country, giving Americans the chance to indulge in an evening's escapade of illicit drinking, and, perhaps, the opportunity to perform the Charleston or black bottom, two of the decade's popular new dances.

It also was a decade of scientific and technological innovation. Medical researchers isolated germs and developed serums that battled such deadly diseases as measles, scarlet fever, and tuberculosis. As the 1920s drew to a close, films that contained speaking and were known as "talkies" forever replaced silent films. Radio was making its way into the ever-growing marketplace. Creative expression reigned in the American arts. A range of new playwrights authored worldly dramas and explored the world's imbalances through witty comedies.

The nightmare of World War I was examined by novelists who created characters that were psychologically damaged by the war. African American artists began expressing their anger at the racism that prevailed in society. Their potent, often eloquent protests were incorporated into the cultural movement called the Harlem Renaissance. Meanwhile, a white separatist group known as the Ku Klux Klan (KKK) wreaked havoc among minorities, and, in particular, blacks, in the American South.

Yet the 1920s was a time of heroes. One of the most heralded was Charles A. Lindbergh, a young aviator who in 1927 completed the first solo transatlantic flight. The decade also was a Golden Age for American sports. Babe Ruth belted home runs in record-breaking numbers for the New York Yankees, which helped distract baseball lovers from the scandal that resulted when eight members of the Chicago White Sox threw the 1919 World Series. College football heroes Harold "Red" Grange and Ernie Nevers were masters of the gridiron. Heavyweight boxing champ Jack Dempsey slugged it out in the ring. Amateur golfer Bobby Jones and tennis player Bill Tilden revolutionized their sports.

The economy in the United States may have been thriving, but politically the country had reverted back to its prewar isolationism. At the beginning of the decade, the government restricted immigration. Foreigners were viewed suspiciously by many native-born Americans. The new Republican Congress had rejected the international peace initiatives proposed by the Democratic president, Woodrow Wilson. Republican Warren G. Harding won a landslide victory in the 1920 presidential election. Republicans held the Oval Office throughout the decade.

As the decade drew to a close, there was no reason to think that the 1930s would be anything less than an extension of the 1920s. Then, one dark day in October 1929, the stock market crashed. This singular event marked the end of the prosperity and good times of the 1920s and ushered in the Great Depression of the 1930s.

chapter one *Arts and Entertainment*

Chronology

1920: Joseph Stella paints *Brooklyn Bridge*.

1920: F. Scott Fitzgerald publishes his first novel, *This Side of Paradise*.

1920: Marcel Duchamp, Man Ray, and Katherine Dreier organize the New York Société Anonyme to promote modern art.

1920: The Julliard Foundation is established in New York to encourage music in the United States.

1920: June 7 *George White's Scandals*, a musical revue, opens on Broadway with songs by George Gershwin.

1920: November 1 *The Emperor Jones*, by Eugene O'Neill, premieres at the Provincetown Playhouse in Greenwich Village.

1921: Poet Edna St. Vincent Millay publishes *Second April*.

1921: Booth Tarkington publishes his novel *Alice Adams*.

1921: *The Love for Three Oranges*, by Sergei Prokofiev, has its world premiere at the Chicago Civic Opera.

1921: *Nanook of the North*, a documentary filmed by Robert Flaherty, premieres in New York City.

1921: James Joyce's *Ulysses* is published in book form.

1921: Poet T. S. Eliot publishes *The Waste Land*.

1921: George Bellows paints *The White House*.

1921: May 23 *Abie's Irish Rose*, a comedy of an intermarriage between an Irish Catholic and a Jew, opens in New York City and runs for a record 2,327 performances.

1923: Robert Frost publishes *New Hampshire*, a collection of his poems.

1923: Rockwell Kent paints *Shadows of Evening*.

1923: February 16 Blues singer Bessie Smith makes her first recordings ("Down Hearted Blues" and "Gulf Coast Blues").

1923: March 19 *The Adding Machine*, an early expressionistic drama by Elmer Rice, opens in New York City.

1923: April 6 Louis Armstrong records his first solo on "Chime Blues" with King Oliver's Creole Jazz Band.

1924: Georgia O'Keeffe paints *Dark Abstraction*.

1924: Michel Fokine forms the American Ballet.

1924: **February 24** *Rhapsody in Blue,* a symphonic composition by George Gershwin, is performed by Paul Whiteman and his orchestra in New York City.

1924: **November 24** *They Knew What They Wanted,* a play by Sidney Howard, opens in New York City.

1925: Man Ray paints *Sugar Loaves.*

1925: Paul Manship sculpts *Flight of Europa.*

1925: **September 21** The operetta, *The Vagabond King,* with music by Rudolf Friml, opens in New York City.

1926: John Barrymore stars in the film *Don Juan.*

1926: Ernest Hemingway's first novel *The Sun Also Rises* is published.

1926: Langston Hughes publishes his first volume of poetry, *The Weary Blues.*

1926: **September 15** Jelly Roll Morton makes his first recordings with the Red Hot Peppers, including "Blackbottom Stomp."

1927: John Gilbert and Greta Garbo co-star in the film *Love.*

1927: **September 8** Bix Beiderbecke records his solo piano classic, "In a Mist."

1927: **October 6** *The Jazz Singer,* starring Al Jolson, premieres in New York City at the Warner Theatre.

1927: **December 27** *Paris Bound,* a play by Philip Barry, opens in New York City.

1928: Djuna Barnes publishes the novel *Ryder.*

1928: Erich von Stroheim directs and stars in the film *The Wedding March.*

1928: *Le Sacre du Printemps* is produced with featured dancer Martha Graham.

1929: Husband and wife Douglas Fairbanks and Mary Pickford co-star in a film version of *The Taming of the Shrew,* by William Shakespeare.

1929: Alexander Calder sculpts *Circus.*

1929: **January 10** *Street Scene,* by Elmer Rice, opens at the Playhouse in New York City.

1929: **November 27** *Fifty Million Frenchmen,* a musical comedy with songs by Cole Porter, premieres in New York City.

Overview

During the 1920s, the arts and media responded and adjusted to shifts in the larger society. World War I had changed America's relation to the world, the American economy boomed after the war, and young people embraced more modern lifestyles. The arts responded to all these social trends. The 1920s was known as the Jazz Age, reflecting the fact that new music and dance styles spread throughout the country. It was also a decade during which young people in particular began embracing a general loosening of morality. For many, the devastation of the war had resulted in a loss of the idealism that was so prevalent during the first part of the century, and the American dream of success was up for re-examination.

In this atmosphere, the theater became fertile ground for exploring serious issues. Playwrights such as Eugene O'Neill and Elmer Rice did so through introspective, earthy dramas; while Ben Hecht, Charles MacArthur, Philip Barry, and George S. Kaufman explored the imbalances of the world through witty comedies.

While Hollywood movies often did not match the standards of the theater for seriously dealing with society's issues, the motion picture industry had quite an exciting decade, too. Many films concentrated on the new attitudes about morality and the effects on traditional domestic lifestyles. Others catered to society's fascination with exotic places. The most dramatic transformation in the motion picture industry, however, was dependent upon technology, not content. As the decade drew to a close, the perfection of new inventions changed movies from "silent films" into "talking pictures."

In literature, too, the Jazz Age brought stories of a discontented generation. There were many portraits of people psychologically damaged by the war, and studies of a generation that was breaking away from traditional American lifestyles that stressed hard work, church attendance, and devotion to the family. African American artists began to express anger at white society's treatment of their race. Their powerful and often eloquent protests became known as the Harlem Renaissance.

In dance, painting, and sculpture, groups of artists banded together in movements to represent objects and express ideas and feelings through realistic as well as abstract approaches. As the fine arts and popular arts flourished, so did the media arts. Radio programming was primitive, but it was finding its way in an ever-growing marketplace. Advertising agencies created catchy product logos to exploit the country's growing consumerism.

Louis Armstrong (1901–1971) Louis Armstrong was the greatest cornet and trumpet player ever. His 1920s recordings with the Hot Five are milestone performances in the history of American jazz. In addition to playing an instrument, Armstrong was an innovative vocalist. With his unique gravelly voice, he sang solos on many recordings. Occasionally Armstrong sang scat songs made up of nonsense syllables instead of words. His recording of "Hello, Dolly!" in the 1960s topped off a long successful career and won him the hearts of a whole new generation of listeners. *Photo reproduced by permission of Schomburg Center for Research in Black Culture.*

F. Scott Fitzgerald (1896–1940) F. Scott Fitzgerald is the American writer most closely tied to the 1920s. He spoke for the post-World War I generation which had lost touch with traditional American ideals. His first novel, *This Side of Paradise* (1920), defined the values of the Jazz Age. In 1925, he published *The Great Gatsby,* a masterpiece of literary style that explores the corruption of the American Dream. Fitzgerald's talents were handicapped by his alcoholism, and his need to work on commercial projects such as movie scripts to raise money to treat his wife Zelda's mental illness. *Photo reproduced courtesy of the Library of Congress.*

George Gershwin (1898–1937) With brother Ira (1896–1983) writing the lyrics, George Gershwin provided the world with a treasure trove of beloved songs, including "Someone to Watch Over Me," "They Can't Take That Away From Me," "Strike Up the Band," and "Our Love Is Here to Stay." As a songplugger (someone who played songs for audiences to get them to buy sheet music) for Tin Pan Alley music companies, twenty-one-year-old Gershwin cowrote his first hit, "Swanee." After penning several dozen popular songs for Broadway shows, he composed symphonic works such as *Rhapsody in Blue* and *An American in Paris,* and the opera *Porgy and Bess* (1935). Gershwin's *Of Thee I Sing* (1931) was the first musical comedy to win a Pulitzer Prize. *Photo reproduced by permission of AP/Wide World Photos.*

Ernest Hemingway (1899–1961) Ernest Hemingway's first novel, *The Sun Also Rises* (1926), gave a name to the generation of expatriates whose experiences in World War I left them passing time aimlessly at Parisian cafes: they were "The Lost Generation." He wrote one classic after another for fifteen years, and after a slip in his literary position, made a comeback with *The Old Man and the Sea* (1952), which helped him to win the Nobel Prize in 1954. Hemingway had a reputation for his personal exploits. He was a hard drinker, a sportsman, and even a journalist in the Spanish Civil War. *Photo reproduced by permission of the Corbis Corporation.*

Al Jolson (1886–1950) Al Jolson was known as "The World's Greatest Entertainer." He starred in Broadway musicals in the 1920s, in which he often played a comical character named Gus in blackface, using make-up to darken his skin. Jolson sang comedy tunes such as "The Spaniard That Blighted My Life" and "Toot, Toot, Tootsie," and sentimental songs such as "My Mammy," "April Showers," "Sonny Boy," and "Avalon." His charismatic performance in *The Jazz Singer* (1927), the first feature-length film with musical numbers and a talking sequence, helped to revolutionize the moving picture industry. *Photo reproduced by permission of AP/Wide World Photos.*

Eugene O'Neill (1888–1953) Eugene O'Neill is one of the most important American playwrights. His plays examine the inner beings of his characters, and they display a solemnity similar to the European dramas of the time. His writing approach was varied, at times using expressionism, naturalism, and symbolism. O'Neill's dramas include *The Emperor Jones* (1920), *Anna Christie* (1921), *Mourning Becomes Electra* (1931), and *Long Day's Journey into Night* (1955). O'Neill won four Pulitzer Prizes for his plays, and he was awarded the Nobel Prize for literature in 1936. *Photo reproduced courtesy of the Library of Congress.*

William S. Paley (1901–1990) One day before his twenty-seventh birthday, William S. Paley and his father invested $300,000 to buy a Philadelphia-based radio station, WCAU, and a controlling interest in the rather unstable United Independent Broadcasters Network. Paley changed the name of the outfit to the Columbia Broadcasting System (CBS), became its president, and spent the next few decades building his asset into a billion-dollar media conglomerate. His programming ideas were very profitable, and he became well known for shaping the content of American radio programming. *Photo reproduced by permission of Archive Photos, Inc.*

David Sarnoff (1891–1971) Russian-born David Sarnoff fulfilled many an immigrant's ideal of the American Dream by becoming a powerful media executive. As sole supporter of his family at age fifteen, he went to work as a messenger boy and then taught himself telegraphy to be able to work at the Marconi Wireless Telegraph Company of America. He went on to become the head of the Radio Corporation of America (RCA), and in 1926 founded the National Broadcasting Company (NBC)—the first commercial radio network. Sarnoff's understanding of the technical aspects of radio, and subsequently television, helped to lay a framework for modern-day in-home media communications. *Photo reproduced by permission of the Corbis Corporation.*

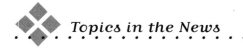

Topics in the News

❖ NEW YORK CITY THEATER

Live theater flourished during the 1920s, with a steady flow of finely written, introspective dramas and fast-paced, cynical comedies from contemporary writers. Theatergoers in New York City could choose from an array of plays staged at various Broadway venues or in the outer neighborhoods, such as Greenwich Village. At the start of the decade, the top playwrights were drawn to the New York stage, which was home to the nation's best dramatic talent. That situation changed, however, with the coming of sound to motion pictures in 1927 and 1928. As the studios made offers of high salaries to the most successful playwrights, creative talent migrated to Los Angeles. That factor, plus the drop in funding for mounting productions as a result of the stock market crash at the end of 1929, ended this cycle of lively activity in the New York theater.

The most memorable dramas and comedies of the decade were works of substance by a number of American playwrights: Maxwell Anderson, George Kelly, Samson Raphaelson, Marc Connelly, Philip Dunning, Elmer Rice, Sidney Howard, George S. Kaufman, Edna Ferber, Ben Hecht, Charles MacArthur, and Philip Barry. Their plays offered perceptive commentary on a variety of topics. Among them were pokes at the eccentricities of the super-rich, social protests against the evils of poverty, searching studies of marriage and family relations, satires about false values, and occasional looks backward to the devastation World War I had left upon society. Often the dramatic approach was realistic; however, there also were flights of fancy. Two effective fantasies were written by Europeans: *Liliom* (1921), by Hungarian playwright Ferenc Molnar (1878–1952), which a quarter-century later inspired the musical *Carousel* (1945), by Richard Rodgers (1902–1981) and Oscar Hammerstein II (1895–1960); and *R.U.R. (Rossom's Universal Robots)* (1922), by Czech playwright Karel Capek (1890–1938), the play that first brought the word "robot" to the English language.

The outstanding dramatic playwright of the decade was Eugene O'Neill (1888–1953), who experimented with new techniques in writing and presentation. He mainly held to realism and naturalism in his approach to his dramas, but he sometimes used symbolism to reinforce his points. O'Neill also employed "expressionism," which distorts speech, action, and setting through simplification, exaggeration, and symbolism. In 1920, his successful drama *The Emperor Jones,* considered the first expressionistic play in the United States, premiered at the Provincetown Playhouse in Greenwich Village. In it, Brutus Jones, the pompous "emperor" of a small

Year	Title	Author
1920	*Beyond the Horizon*	Eugene O'Neill
1921	*Miss Lulu Bett*	Zona Gale
1922	*Anna Christie*	Eugene O'Neill
1923	*Icebound*	Owen Davis
1924	*Hell-Bent for Heaven*	Hatcher Hughes
1925	*They Knew What They Wanted*	Sidney Howard
1926	*Craig's Wife*	George Kelly
1927	*In Abraham's Bosom*	Paul Green
1928	*Strange Interlude*	Eugene O'Neill
1929	*Street Scene*	Elmer Rice

West Indies Island, escapes through the forest when he is removed from his throne. As he runs, Jones sees strange visions, fears for his life, and reverts to humanity's primitive nature. Throughout the decade, O'Neill continued to offer plays that have remained classics.

❖ MUSICAL THEATER

Musical variety shows called revues continued to provide entertainment to Americans on Broadway and in theaters across the country. Each year, Florenz Ziegfeld (1867–1932) produced his elaborate *Follies.* Other annual revues included: *George White's Scandals,* with songs by George (1898–1937) and Ira (1896–1981) Gershwin, performed during the first half of the decade; *The Music Box Revue,* featuring songs by Irving Berlin (1888–1989); *The Earl Carroll Vanities;* and *The Greenwich Village Follies.*

Musical comedies also were abundant during the decade, and they acquainted audiences with a stream of talented performers who would become successes in talking motion pictures. The musical stage comedy *I'll Say She Is!* introduced the zany comedy team of the Marx Brothers in 1924. Future movie star Fred Astaire (1899–1987) entertained audiences in a string of hit musicals, as did Eddie Cantor, Al Jolson, Bert Lahr, Ethel Merman, Helen Morgan, W. C. Fields, and Will Rogers. Also, a number of chorus members would find success in motion pictures at the close of the decade: Ruby Keeler, Ginger Rogers, Barbara Stanwyck, Paulette Goddard, and even James Cagney—who later became a major star in serious roles.

By the late 1920s, Busby Berkeley (1895–1976) was considered the top dance director of the New York stage. He, too, would join the migration to Hollywood and become a major director of musical films.

The most significant musical show of the decade was *Showboat* (1927), based on a novel by Edna Ferber (1887–1968). Before *Showboat,* the plots of musicals generally were thin and lightweight. Here, however, the story was meaty and controversial. It related the tale of a young showboat entertainer who loves a riverboat gambler, and the play had subplots about interracial relations. Because the songs were integrated into the dramatic action, *Showboat* took a step forward from its predecessors and paved the way for the modern American musical genre.

❖ THE HARLEM RENAISSANCE

During the early part of the 1920s, a number of gifted, educated African Americans gravitated to Harlem, the neighborhood north of 125th Street in New York City where many blacks lived. This group included dramatists, poets, novelists, composers, and musicians who became the voice of the Harlem Renaissance, a term first mentioned in a 1925 article in the *New York Herald Tribune* to describe the tremendous creative activity going on in the African American community. During this time, black writing changed from works in Negro dialect and imitations of white writing to creations that expressed black culture and protest. Because a number of white people traveled to Harlem to share the nightlife in the many clubs, the Harlem Renaissance also received attention in the white media.

The movement was shaped by Alain Locke (1886–1954), a Howard University philosopher and the first black Rhodes Scholar who had published many thought-provoking essays in a publication he edited called *The New Negro;* and Carl Van Vechten (1880–1964), a white editor and patron of the arts who was friends with many black writers of the day. Langston Hughes (1902–1967), known as the "poet laureate of the Negro race," published his first volume of poetry, *The Weary Blues,* in 1926. His poems were stark and brutal visions of the poverty and anger felt by black Americans. Hughes is the most important literary figure of the Harlem Renaissance as well as an important, enduring figure in American poetry.

Other writers whose works are key to the movement are poet Countee Cullen (1903–1946), whose work *Color* (1925) encourages taking pride in African roots, and Jean Toomer (1894–1967) whose *Cane* (1923) is consid-

The dance craze of the era was The Charleston, a high-stepping, jazzy dance for flappers and their male partners. "The Charleston" originated as a dance song by James P. Johnson (1891–1955) and Cecil Mack (1883–1944). It debuted in 1923 in *Runnin Wild,* an all-black musical show in New York City. The freewheeling dance was inspired by the movements of African American dancers in Charleston, South Carolina. It was fast-paced and boldly athletic, a change from the ladylike movements of couple-dancing. What's more, if the flapper wore a short skirt with fringe and rolled stockings, a lucky young man could catch a glimpse of his partner's bare thighs.

ered the first novel of the Harlem Renaissance. In 1928, Jamaican writer Claude McKay (1890–1948) published *Home to Harlem,* a gritty novel of black life whose militarism incited anger in more moderate African American leaders such as W.E.B. Du Bois (1868–1963) and Alain Locke. Nevertheless, *Home to Harlem* was highly praised and won awards. A number of female voices also emerged from the Harlem Renaissance, including writers Jessie Fauset, Nella Larson, and Zora Neale Hurston.

The Harlem Renaissance also had an impact on music. In 1921, an all-black musical *Shuffle Along* opened at the Sixty-Third Street Theatre, a rather tumble-down venue that was separated by several blocks from more established theaters in Manhattan. The score was written by Noble Sissle (1889–1975) and Eubie Blake (1883–1983), and spawned two hit songs, "I'm Just Wild about Harry" and "Love Will Find a Way." Even though the show did not receive much funding at first, due in part to racial prejudices, it received several good reviews and many theatergoers trekked uptown to see it during its 504-performance run. The unexpected success of *Shuffle Along* helped to make black shows fashionable during the 1920s.

❖ JAZZ

During the first few years of the twentieth century, the term "jazz" was used to describe a type of African American Creole music played by brass bands in the rough-sections of New Orleans. One pre-World War I definition of the term was a synonym for sexual intercourse! By the 1910s, black musicians across parts of the South and in Chicago were demonstrating a much broader interest in jazz music, setting up centers of jazz culture where musicians experimented with innovative ways to write and play jazz compositions. A number of composers and performers of popular songs—particularly Russian Jews such as Irving Berlin, George Gershwin, Al Jolson, and Sophie Tucker—were incorporating jazz touches into their music.

What is jazz? It is an American style of music, inspired mainly by African American slave music and characterized by syncopated rhythms, distortions of pitch and timber, and some improvisation (playing without written music). Syncopated music involves displacing the accent from the regular metered beat and temporarily placing the accent on the weak beats. By the mid-1920s, symphonic composers such as Virgil Thompson and Aaron Copland, culture critic Gilbert Seldes, bandleaders John Philip Sousa, Paul Whiteman, and Vincent Lopez, and a host of other Americans were writing essays on the definition, origins, and meaning of jazz. If this type of music was not yet considered mainstream, at least it was a main topic of conversation among the musical literati (the intellectual elite of musical studies).

Among the most famous jazz musicians of the decade were a group of African Americans. Louis Armstrong (1901–1971) is considered by many as the greatest trumpet player ever. In 1922, he was playing cornet with King Oliver's Creole Jazz Band in Chicago. Two years later, he joined the Fletcher Henderson Orchestra in New York. Then in 1925, he formed his own jazz group, the Hot Five, which was a studio ensemble that produced 78-rpm vinyl records, some of which included Armstrong's distinctive gravelly singing voice, to be marketed especially to southern blacks. Since most Americans during the decade owned phonographs which could play these records, Armstrong soon found a large audience for his music. He became the most famous black musical entertainer of the period, eventually appealing to white music lovers, too.

Another notable black artist of the 1920s is Bessie Smith (1894–1937), one of the country's greatest blues singers. Blues was a style of jazz music first popularized by W. C. Handy (1873–1958) in the early years of the century; its songs repeat soulful moans or laments. Smith's lusty voice cried sad, fatalistic songs of misery. She toured the South with other black performers and made 160 recordings, which at that time appealed mainly to an African American audience. By the end of the decade, Smith lost popularity as more innovative forms of jazz made her traditional blues singing seem outdated.

Jelly Roll Morton (1885–1941) was an important jazz composer and pianist who claimed that he actually had invented jazz in 1902. While that

Pulitzer Prizes for Fiction.

Year	Title	Author
1920	No award	
1921	*The Age of Innocence*	Edith Wharton
1922	*Alice Adams*	Booth Tarkington
1923	*One of Ours*	Willa Cather
1924	*The Able McLaughlins*	Margaret Wilson
1925	*So Big*	Edna Ferber
1926	*Arrowsmith*	Sinclair Lewis (declined)
1927	*Early Autumn*	Louis Bromfield
1928	*The Bridge of San Luis Rey*	Thornton Wilder
1929	*Scarlet Sister Mary*	Julia Peterkin

was not true, he did think up a number of complex rhythms and musical flourishes that were innovative. Bix Beiderbecke (1903–1931) lived a relatively brief life, but he nevertheless became one of the most important jazz musicians of the era. A proponent of the Chicago jazz scene, he was a jazz pianist and has been called the greatest white trumpet player of all time.

❖ EXPATRIATES AND LITERARY MOVEMENTS

During the decade, the seat of American literature actually appeared to be located in Paris, on the Left Bank of the Seine river. A colony of American writers settled there after World War I, and many stayed in Paris through the 1920s. Among the expatriates (those who leave their country to live in another) were a mixture of up-and-coming and renowned novelists, short-story writers, and poets: Ernest Hemingway, F. Scott Fitzgerald, Gertrude Stein, Ezra Pound, Djuna Barnes, Kay Boyle, e.e. cummings, Hilda Doolittle (also known as H.D.), Janet Flanner, and Archibald MacLeish. These writers were joined by expatriate American artists such as Man Ray, Alexander Calder, and Jo Davidson.

Not all the American artists who set up residence in Paris were productive. Many of them formed a "Lost Generation," a term coined by Gertrude Stein (1874–1946) and quoted by Hemingway (1899–1961) in his novel *The Sun Also Rises* (1926). There were many young American artists whose creative philosophies were muddled by the events of the war, and who no longer could manage a clear sense of the world. They often lived on monetary donations from friends and family, spending their time drinking at Parisian cafes. Some were memorialized as subjects in the works of the more prolific and successful expatriate writers.

Writers during the 1920s continued to develop a modernist literary movement, which rejected traditional technique and morality and focused on the plight of the individual in an insensitive, mechanized, and commercial world. Perhaps the strongest influence on innovative English-language writing during the decade was the novel *Ulysses*, by Irish writer James Joyce (1882–1941), which had been published in magazine installments in the late 1910s but finally was published in book form in 1922. In *Ulysses*, Joyce uses a writing technique known as stream-of-consciousness to explore the inner lives of his characters, and he even concocts a type of private language. Many readers had trouble digesting this new style of writing, and it never caught on as a generally used literary style. However, American novelist John Dos Passos (1896–1970) adapted Joyce's techniques for *Manhattan Transfer* (1925), a patchwork quilt of episodes that convey a sense of New York City.

Another literary movement was building among southern writers during the decade. In 1920, the majority of southern novelists wrote about their region in terms of its pre-Civil War "Old South" traditions. Richmond, Virginia-based novelists James Branch Cabell (1879–1958) and Ellen Glasgow (1873–1945) launched an attack on the old southern school of writing and urged their colleagues to find new ways of treating southern material. The resulting new forms of writing became part of a movement known as the Southern Renaissance. Its greatest figure was William Faulkner (1897–1962), who found inventive ways to write about the traditional themes of the Civil War, the collapse of the old southern aristocracy, and the effects of commercialism on southern lifestyles.

❖ MOTION PICTURES

Hollywood movies have often reflected society. As such, the movies of the post-World War I Jazz Age spoke to the newly adopted values and philosophies of American audiences. The younger generation of Americans had been most affected by the war; many citizens born into the twentieth century believed in a new morality, including new freedoms for women and the acceptance of the party-loving "flapper" or "jazz baby." Whereas their parents believed that rural life was pure and that the city was a den of sin, young people of the decade viewed the big cities—with

A woman performing the Charleston. The new dance was so popular during the 1920s that Joan Crawford even performed it during the film Our Dancing Daughters. *Reproduced by permission of the Corbis Corporation.*

their tall buildings, anonymous crowds, and potential for fame and wealth—as places of unending excitement. Many films of the 1920s sought to bring these new thoughts and morality to the screen.

One of the best examples of the Jazz Age movie is *It* (1927), based on the book by Elinor Glyn (1864–1943), about a spirited salesgirl who has romantic feelings for her boss. Its perky star, Clara Bow (1905–1965), became known as "The It Girl." "It" became a term for undefinable sex appeal. Another of the genre is *Our Dancing Daughters* (1928), the story of a rich, party-loving flapper whose boyfriend is manipulated into marrying a more old-fashioned sort of woman. In this film, star Joan Crawford (1904–1977) performs the Charleston, the most popular new dance of the decade.

Additionally, there was a postwar spirit of exploration that inspired many films about adventures in exotic places. Stories transported moviegoers from the windswept Sahara Desert to the North Pole. Documentaries captivated audiences: examples are *Nanook of the North* (1922), shot in the Hudson Bay region, and *Chang: A Drama of the Wilderness* (1927), shot in the jungles of Siam, which now is Thailand.

Two popular romantic adventure stories that combined the new morality with exotic locales starred romantic heartthrob Rudolph Valentino (1895–1926) as *The Sheik* (1921) and *Son of the Sheik* (1926). Valentino's hot-blooded moves may be laughable to current audiences, but they demonstrated a new sensuality that entered American films during the 1920s.

❖ TALKING PICTURES

For most of the decade, movies were "silent films." They actually were shown with accompanying piano scores, or even full orchestral accompaniment in big city movie palaces (huge, elaborate theaters often designed with Oriental or other exotic themes). Attempts were made to add recorded soundtracks to motion pictures, but there were problems with synchronizing picture and sound and with amplifying the sound. By the mid-1920s, two systems had been perfected. One was called the Movietone system, with a soundtrack laid right onto the strip of film. The other was the Vitaphone system, which relied on the playing of a large vinyl disc on a special phonograph machine that worked in concert with the film projector. Feature films such as *Don Juan* (1926) began to be made with synchronized music and effects, and short films even featured performers talking and singing.

Even so, very few theaters committed to installing sound equipment until a then-fairly insignificant studio named Warner Bros. produced *The Jazz Singer*, a feature-length melodrama with musical numbers, in the summer of 1927. The film tells the story of the son of a devout Jewish cantor (a religious official who leads musical parts of worship services) forsaking his traditional role as the next-generation cantor in order to pursue a secular life as a jazz vocalist. The movie featured Al Jolson (1886–1950), the country's most popular musical stage star. Enthusiastic audiences flocked to theaters to see their favorite entertainer in a sound film. Actually, aside from the singing scenes, there was only one scene featuring dialogue; in it, Jolson has an extended conversation with his mother. Yet this

1927 to 1928

Actor:	Emil Jannings, *The Way of All Flesh* and *The Last Command*
Actress:	Janet Gaynor, *Seventh Heaven*, *Street Angel* and *Sunrise*
Director:	Frank Borzage, *Seventh Heaven* and Lewis Milestone, *Two Arabian Nights*
Picture:	*Wings*

1928 to 1929

Actor:	Warner Baxter, *In Old Arizona*
Actress:	Mary Pickford, *Coquette*
Director:	Frank Lloyd, *Divine Lady*
Picture:	*The Broadway Melody*

1929 to 1930

Actor:	George Arliss, *Disraeli*
Actress:	Norma Shearer, *The Divorcee*
Director:	Lewis Milestone, *All Quiet on the Western Front*
Picture:	*All Quiet on the Western Front*

film was so successful that audiences clamored to *hear* as well as to see motion pictures. Within a year or two, most theaters across the nation were fitted with sound systems, making silent films a thing of the past. By the end of 1929, studios advertised that their movies were "all singing, all dancing, all talking."

❖ PAINTING

Several schools of American modern art dominated the 1920s. The "Ash Can School," named for a painting by John Sloan (1871–1951) of a woman rummaging through a trash can, included realistic paintings of informal, sometimes downright seedy, subjects. Sloan, along with George Bellows (1882–1925), continued to produce important work during the decade. Cubism, a form of abstract art that stresses color, texture, and construction in collage, remained popular, particularly among a group of American artists who were influenced by photographer and editor Alfred Stieglitz (1864–1946), the founder of Gallery 291 in New York City. Precisionism (also known as Cubist Realism or Cubo-Realism) presented subjects with accuracy or realism, but with a simplicity that achieved an abstract effect. Georgia O'Keeffe (1887–1986), who was married to Stieglitz, was associated with this school, as her close-up studies of flowers and plants attest. So were Charles Sheeler (1883–1965) and Charles Demuth (1883–1935). Sheeler had an austere style, exemplified by his painting *Upper Deck* (1929). Demuth painted in a variety of styles, but in the 1920s he was a precisionist, as can be seen in his *Industry* (c. 1924) and *My Egypt* (1927).

New Orleans-born painter Archibald Motley Jr. (1891–1981) held a special place in the decade's art scene. He decided to paint in abstract forms while studying in Paris, and he was the first African American artist to have a solo exhibition of his works in a commercial gallery.

Edward Hopper (1882–1967) and Charles Burchfield (1893–1967) were realist painters who also enjoyed success during the decade. Hopper's paintings, such as *House by the Railroad* (1921), offer a sense of isolation and loneliness. Burchfield's work portrays the natural world with touches of evil and hostility, evident in his *House of Mystery* (1924).

❖ ADVERTISING AND PUBLIC RELATIONS

After the war, there was a boom in consumerism. With the public scurrying around to find the most appealing vacuum cleaner, dress shirt, automobile, or bath soap, the advertising industry expanded to meet the needs of product manufacturers. One of the most powerful advertising agencies, J. Walter Thompson, billed out $10.7 million to clients in 1922; in 1929 it billed out $37.5 million.

The age of the advertising slogan had arrived. Lucky Strike (cigarettes) urged women to "Reach for a Lucky instead of a sweet," during a decade when few respectable women smoked in public. Woodbury facial soap was "For the skin you love to touch," while Palmolive soap would help its users "Keep that schoolgirl complexion." And one should use Listerine mouthwash to stop bad breath when "Even your best friend won't tell you."

❖ FAN MAGAZINES, PULP FICTION, AND HARD-BOILED DETECTIVES

A variety of different magazines appeared in the 1920s to satisfy every possible audience. Fan magazines had been available to motion picture enthusiasts during the previous decade, but the 1920s brought a more provocative type of movie star magazine to the public. These periodicals carried stories of wild parties, romantic entanglements, and star jealousies. The popular titles included *Photoplay, Screenland,* and *Screen Romances.*

Captain Billy's Whiz Bang began in 1919 as a joke sheet that sold in hotel lobbies for 25 cents. The man behind Captain Billy was Wilford H. Fawcett (?–1940); a whiz bang was the slang term for a World War I shell. Captain Billy's jokes were lewd, and the stories contained plenty of outhouse humor. Even so, by the mid-1920s, each issue was selling nearly a half million copies. This objectionable periodical was so successful that profits from its sale laid the foundation for the Fawcett publishing empire of magazines and paperback books.

The appeal of "hard-boiled" or realistic, sometimes gory detective stories spanned the decade. Because these fictions were published on cheap wood-pulp paper, they gained the nickname "pulps." The best and most famous magazine in the genre was *Black Mask.* In it, author Raymond Chandler (1888–1959) published stories of tough characters, writing with a fast-paced wit.

Dashiell Hammett (1894–1961), a former Pinkerton detective, published stories in *Black Mask* beginning in 1922. In one of the pioneering moves toward making pulp fiction respectable, several of Hammett's stories about a detective identified only as the Continental Op (short for operative, a word meaning detective) were published by an imprint of Alfred A. Knopf, along with Hammett's first novel, *Red Harvest* (1929).

For More Information

BOOKS

Applebaum, Stanley, ed. *The New York Stage: Famous Productions in Photographs.* New York: Dover Publications, 1976.

Berry, Michael. *Georgia O'Keeffe.* New York: Chelsea House, 1988.

Bloom, Harold, ed. *Ernest Hemingway.* Philadelphia: Chelsea House, 2001.

Bloom, Harold, ed. *F. Scott Fitzgerald.* Philadelphia: Chelsea House, 2000.

Bloom, Harold, ed. *James Joyce.* Philadelphia: Chelsea House, 2001.

Blum, Daniel. *Great Stars of the American Stage.* New York: Grosset & Dunlap, 1952.

Blum, Daniel, enlarged by John Willis. *A Pictorial History of the American Theatre,* 6th edition. New York: Crown Publishers, 1986.

Blum, Daniel. *A Pictorial History of the Silent Screen.* New York: Putnam, 1953.

Buxton, Frank, and Bill Owen. *The Big Broadcast, 1920–1950*. New York: The Viking Press, 1966.

Candaele, Kerry. *Bound for Glory 1910–1930: From the Great Migration to the Harlem Renaissance*. New York: Chelsea House, 1996.

Collins, David R. *Bix Beiderbecke: Jazz Age Genius*. Greensboro, NC: Morgan Reynolds, 1998.

Daffron, Carolyn. *Edna St. Vincent Millay*. New York: Chelsea House, 1989.

Finkelstein, Norman H. *Sounds of the Air: The Golden Age of Radio*. New York: Charles Scribner's, 1993.

Freedman, Russell. *Martha Graham: A Dancer's Life*. New York: Clarion, 1998.

Gottfried, Ted. *The American Media*. New York: Franklin Watts, 1997.

Halliwell, Sarah, ed. *The 20th Century: Pre–1945 Artists, Writers, and Composers*. Austin, TX: Raintree Steck-Vaughn, 1998.

Hardy, P. Stephen, and Sheila Jackson Hardy. *Extraordinary People of the Harlem Renaissance*. New York: Children's Press, 2000.

Haskins, James. *The Harlem Renaissance*. Brookfield, CT: Millbrook Press, 1996.

Hill, Christine. *Langston Hughes: Poet of the Harlem Renaissance*. Springfield, NJ: Enslow Publishers, 1997.

Jacques, Geoffrey. *Free Within Ourselves: The Harlem Renaissance*. New York: Franklin Watts, 1996.

Janson, H.W., and Anthony F. Janson. *History of Art for Young People*, 5th edition. New York: Harry Abrams, 1997.

Katz, Ephraim. *The Film Encyclopedia*, 4th edition. New York: HarperResource, 2001.

Kreuger, Miles. *Show Boat: The Story of a Classic American Musical*. New York: Applause, 1995.

Maltin, Leonard. *The Great American Broadcast*. New York: Dutton, 1997.

Maltin, Leonard, ed. *Leonard Maltin's Movie Encyclopedia*. New York: Dutton, 1994.

Meltzer, Milton. *Langston Hughes*. Brookfield, CT: Millbrook Press, 1997.

Munden, Kenneth W., executive ed. *The American Film Institute Catalog of Motion Pictures Produced in the United States, Feature Films, 1921–1930*. New York, R.R. Bowker, 1971.

Orgill, Roxane. *If I Only Had a Horn: Young Louis Armstrong*. Boston: Houghton Mifflin, 1997.

Orgill, Roxane. *Shout, Sister, Shout! Ten Girl Singers Who Shaped a Century*. New York: Margaret McElderry, 2001.

Pietrusza, David. *The Roaring Twenties*. San Diego: Lucent, 1998.

Reef, Catherine. *George Gershwin: American Composer*. Greensboro, NC: Morgan Reynolds, 2000.

Tessitore, John. *F. Scott Fitzgerald: The American Dreamer*. New York: Franklin Watts, 2001.

Tessitore, John. *The Hunt and the Feast: A Life of Ernest Hemingway.* New York: Franklin Watts, 1996.

Vaughan, William H. T. *Encyclopedia of Artists.* New York: Oxford University Press, 2000.

Yannuzzi, Della A. *Ernest Hemingway: Writer and Adventurer.* Springfield, NJ: Enslow Publishers, 1998.

Yannuzzi, Della A. *Zora Neale Hurston: Southern Story Teller.* Springfield, NJ: Enslow Publishers, 1996.

WEB SITES

Greatest Films of the 1920s. http://www.filmsite.org/20sintro.html (accessed on August 5, 2002).

Media History Timeline: 1920s. http://www.mediahistory.umn.edu/time/1920s.html (accessed on August 5, 2002).

1920s. http://www.richland2.org/svh/Media/socstud/1920s.htm (accessed on August 5, 2002).

1920s Oscar winners. http://www.ew.com/ew/oscar2000/history/1920.html (accessed on August 2, 2002).

Business and the Economy

1920: **January 16** Prohibition begins. The manufacture, sale, or transportation of intoxicating liquors in the United States is now illegal.

1920: **February 28** The Esch-Cummins Act restores railroads to private ownership and sets up the Railroad Labor Board.

1921: Following the actions of administrators at the University of Pennsylvania, faculty and staff members establish business schools at Dartmouth College, the University of Chicago, Harvard University, and other major colleges.

1921: The Women's Bureau, a division of the Labor Department, reports that eight million women are in the labor force, 80 percent of them performing clerical work.

1921: **May 10** The Ford Motor Company announces assets of more than $345 million.

1922: Standard Oil announces an eight-hour day for oil field workers.

1922: **July 1** The Railroad Labor Board announces a 13 percent cut in wages, affecting four hundred thousand workers.

1922: **September 19** Congress passes the Fordney-McCumber Tariff Act which lowers tariffs (taxes on imported and exported goods) to the levels of the 1909 Payne-Aldrich Act.

1923: Zenith Radio is founded in Chicago, Illinois.

1923: In order to make Chevrolet cars more competitive with Ford models, General Motors puts its Chevrolet Division under the direction of a former Ford executive.

1923: The Ethyl Corporation introduces a fuel additive to eliminate "knock" and reduce lead deposits in automobile engines.

1924: A&P operates 11,913 grocery stores throughout the United States.

1924: Wall Street booms as 2.2 million shares are traded on the stock exchange.

1924: Union Carbide and Carbon Company introduces Prestone, an automobile antifreeze that sells for $5 per gallon.

1924: Ford announces that it has ten thousand dealerships across the nation.

1924: **June** Chrysler Corporation is founded; the automaker's new car sells for approximately $1,500.

1924: **November 30** A wireless transmitter made by the Radio Corporation of America (RCA) sends photos from London to New York City.

1925: **January 17** Addressing the Society of American Newspaper Editors, President Calvin Coolidge states, "The business of America is business."

1925: **February 28** Congress enacts the Corrupt Practices Act which makes it "unlawful for any national bank, or any corporation...to make a contribution or expenditure in connection with any election to any political office." Individual donors are allowed contributions of up to $5,000.

1926: Sears Roebuck distributes fifteen million catalogs and twenty-three million special announcements per year to its customers.

1926: Greyhound Corporation begins bus service on American roads. General Motors is its major stockholder.

1927: RCA splits into two networks, the Red and the Blue, to bring greater efficiency to management.

1927: Chrysler introduces the Plymouth car line, and soon afterward the new division introduces the mid-priced DeSoto sedan.

1927: **May 27** Aviator Charles A. Lindbergh arrives in Paris, France after his 331/2 hour solo flight across the Atlantic Ocean. This feat earns more attention than almost any other event of the decade.

1927: **November** The Model A automobile is introduced by the Ford Motor Company.

1928: A. P. Giannini founds the TransAmerica Corporation.

1928: David Gerber begins selling his improved baby foods in grocery stores.

1928: **January 7** Optimism about the power of American business, called "Coolidge optimism," spurs a stock market boom on Wall Street.

1929: **February 23** The Brotherhood of Sleeping Car Porters, headed by A. Philip Randolph, is the first African-American union to be chartered by the American Federation of Labor (AFL).

1929: **March 17** General Motors announces plans to buy the German automobile firm Opel.

1929: **July 7** Transcontinental Air Transport announces a plan to offer coast-to-coast air and rail service, using airplanes over flatlands and railroad cars in the mountains.

1929: **September 11** The Fokker F32, the world's largest passenger plane, is unveiled.

Overview

The economic conditions of the early 1920s were a direct result of the business conditions that had developed during World War I (1914–18). There were two phases of U.S. participation in the war: first, the United States supplied goods and services to the Allied European nations; later, when the United States joined the war on the side of the Allies, it provided both economic assistance and combat troops. In general, the war benefited American business and the economy. The United States went from isolationism (staying away from involvement in international trade and politics) to become an international trader and banker. Additionally, the increased need created by the war for American products and services had a positive impact on employment, and the need for food abroad provided a similar boost to the agricultural industry.

When the war ended, certain industries remained stable, and others changed significantly. Demand for consumer products such as automobiles and radios not only continued, but grew quickly. This growth accompanied continued development of new technologies. The automobile industry grew more powerful and sophisticated, and it attracted investment from the nation's most influential financiers. The radio industry grew into a commercial marketplace as news and information reports were increasingly overshadowed by highly popular entertainment programs. Meanwhile, firms in all industries recognized the power of radio advertising.

The U.S. aircraft industry would not be transformed from military to commercial for several years. Former World War I pilots first used their skills to perform airplane stunts at local fairs; it would be years before the financial world invested in commercial aircraft manufacturing and airline transportation. Meanwhile, smaller metal and chemical industries that had supplied war-related products made smooth transitions to consumer goods. Because so many domestic products were discontinued during the war in favor of military needs, there was an enthusiastic market demand for hardware and household goods.

With a nation of eager consumers and a prospering economy, employment was high and so was consumer spending. The construction industry flourished in cities and especially in the suburbs, where entire communities were springing up. With so many automobiles sold, hundreds of thousands of middle-working-class American families could live in the suburbs and drive their cars or take newly designed public transportation to their jobs in the cities. The new suburban areas needed schools, shopping areas, and civic buildings, and so the construction field and all of its related industries prospered.

The only group that did not share in the country's economic abundance was the agriculture industry. Farmers expanded their production during the war to sell their crops to embattled countries in Europe. They added high-priced land and more modern equipment by borrowing money from banks. When the European countries regained their ability to grow their own food, the American farmer lost the international market. As a result, masses of farmers could not pay back their bank loans, and many merchants that depended upon farm customers went out of business.

While the administration of Woodrow Wilson participated in the regulation of industry, the subsequent administration of Warren G. Harding, which came into office in 1921, took an attitude of "laissez-faire" (a doctrine opposing government involvement in economic matters), leaving business and industry with few restraints. When President Harding died, his successor, Calvin Coolidge, was somewhat more cautious about industrial policies that were so unconstrained, but his attitude toward business still mirrored Harding's in many ways.

As the decade moved towards its close, a few economists and investors became concerned about the free-wheeling policies of the investment market. Overall, prosperity and unregulated business had led to a very active and volatile stock market. That situation plus a lack of clear banking practices to protect investments eventually caused a stock market crash in October 1929 that would halt the prosperity of the decade and bring about the Great Depression of the 1930s.

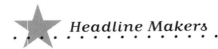
Roger W. Babson (1875–1967) Roger W. Babson became famous as one of just a few people who predicted the 1929 stock market crash. His forecasting methods included charts, graphs, and intersecting lines, but they showed very little scientific knowledge. In fact, despite Babson's claims of being an educator, philosopher, theologian, statistician, economist, and forecaster, his background remains a mystery. After his prophecy came true, he attracted a following in the financial world, and lectured and wrote under the auspices of his Babson Institute and School of Management.

Walter P. Chrysler (1881–1948) Walter Chrysler started his career as a machinist and rose to become one of the important automobile executives of the 1920s. After briefly retiring as president of Buick and vice president of General Motors, he returned to the industry to take over the troubled Willys-Overland Company. Then he moved to the Maxwell Motor Company, renamed it Chrysler Corporation, and in 1925 produced the automobile that would be his namesake.

Donald W. Douglas (1892–1981) Donald Douglas's inspiration for becoming an aeronautical engineer came from pioneer aviator-inventors Orville (1871–1948) and Wilbur (1867–1912) Wright. After working on the development of heavy bomber planes, he developed the *Cloudster,* designed to carry a load exceeding its own weight across the country, although it never actually did so. In the early 1930s, Douglas's DC-3 aircraft, in its passenger and military versions, was noted for outstanding endurance and reliability; the plane still is flown in some parts of the world.

Pierre S. Du Pont (1870–1954) Entrepreneur Pierre S. Du Pont was born into a chemical, gunpowder, and banking dynasty. With his brothers, he reorganized the family business in 1902, and went on to actively manage the Du Pont Company, which flourished as a supplier to the U.S. military during World War I. After the war, the company exploited valuable dye-trust patents confiscated by the U.S. government from Germany. With so much cash available to him, Du Pont also invested in many other companies, most significantly General Motors (GM). Du Pont and his family took control of GM in 1920, and they made sure that GM purchased its vast supplies of paint, finishes, man-made fabrics, and other materials from the Du Pont Company! *Photo reproduced by permission of Archive Photos, Inc.*

Henry Ford (1863–1947) Nobody is more single-handedly responsible for making the motor car available to the American public than Henry Ford. He was a self-taught mechanical genius and the most famous automobile designer and manufacturer of the twentieth century. He produced the first Model T Ford in 1908, and in order to sell this inexpensive but durable car to the maximum number of potential customers, he revolutionized factory work methods by creating and implementing the modern assembly line. During the nineteen years the model was on the market, seventeen million Model Ts were sold!

Amadeo Peter Giannini (1870–1949) Italian American Amadeo Peter Giannini was a leader in the banking world and the founder of the Bank of America. He also financially supported many worthy causes, particularly those in his native state of California and specifically the University of California, Berkeley. In the early 1900s he converted his San Francisco-based family produce business into a small bank. After a devastating earthquake obliterated the heart of the city in 1906, Giannini's Bank of Italy loaned $80,000 to San Francisco concerns that could not obtain financing from the larger local banks, whose assets were destroyed or hidden under the rubble. Soon, the Bank of Italy grew to become the Bank of America. *Photo reproduced courtesy of the Library of Congress.*

Edward V. Rickenbacker (1890–1973) During World War I Eddie Rickenbacker gained a reputation as a flying ace. After the war, his enthusiasm for developing commercial aviation was squelched by financiers, and so he entered the automobile industry. For seven years, he produced the dependable Rickenbacker auto, marketed as "a car worthy of the name." When he finally was able to secure a major financial interest in Eastern Airlines in 1934, Rickenbacker's careful management turned the corporation into one of the most well-run, progressive airlines in the world. *Photo reproduced by permission of AP/Wide World Photos.*

Benjamin Strong (1872–1928) As governor of the New York Central Reserve Bank from 1914 until his death, Benjamin Strong was considered one of the nation's preeminent central bankers. While most of his banking policies were conservative, his decisions during the 1920s remain controversial. His employment of "open-market powers" for Federal Reserve monies, making those funds available for investment in the securities market and in foreign trade, spurred business activity and increased stock market investments. However, these policies also may have brought on the 1929 stock market crash. As a result, Strong's reputation has been tarnished; he is remembered as a mismanager of money in the 1920s. *Photo reproduced by permission of the Corbis Corporation.*

Topics in the News . . . .

❖ INTERCITY TRANSPORTATION

When the decade began, railroads provided the most important form of transportation for people and freight. Since the late nineteenth century, railroad cars had carried passengers from coast to coast and to points in between, and freight cars had handled bulk shipments of every kind of goods. Railroads were a significant factor in the development of the American West. For decades, the U.S. railroad industry was treated as a virtual monopoly (an entity that enjoys exclusive ownership through legal privilege) on intercity transportation. The railroad system was so key to the success of the U.S. war effort in 1917 and 1918 that the federal government actually took control of the industry and did not return it to private ownership until 1921.

During the 1920s, optimism about the future of railroad usage caused management to invest more than $6 million in facilities and equipment. What the railroad executives failed to foresee was the growing importance of automobiles, trucks, buses, and airplanes in transporting people and products to all parts of the country. The decline in the use of railroads was a fairly difficult trend to detect in the early 1920s, when passenger service revenue dropped from $1.2 million to $876 thousand but freight revenue actually rose from $4.4 million to $4.8 million. By the end of the decade, however, both services were in a slight decline.

At the start of the decade, automobiles and trucks were slowly gaining a foothold in the intercity transportation industry. These vehicles would have taken a greater chunk of business away from the railroad industry if there had been an adequate system of roads; however, most U.S. roads still were unpaved and deeply rutted from wagon wheels. Rain caused many automobiles to get stuck in slippery mud and deep grooves; in fact, a number of early car companies advertised the ability of their product to operate under these primitive road conditions.

The lack of modern roads prompted the federal government in 1916 to take responsibility for financing and constructing intercounty and interstate road systems, to be built according to a national standard. Thus the 1920s became a decade of road construction. Such major thoroughfares as U.S. Highway 1, U.S. Highway 50, and U.S. Interstate 66 became key interstate transportation routes and spawned the construction of many branch roads. Aside from the issue of road conditions, the use of trucks and buses for intercity transportation was limited by the actual design of those vehicles. Trucks of the 1920s basically were larger versions of automobiles, and the tractor-trailer was in a pioneering stage. Buses, too, were built less substantially than they would be in the 1930s, and commercial bus lines of the decade were small enterprises that were in effect "mom and pop" operations. With these limitations, trucks and buses generally were used only for short trips during the 1920s.

World War I brought the attention of the American public to airplane carriers; it was not until 1927, however, with the highly publicized transatlantic flight of Charles Lindbergh (1902–1974), that Americans began to imagine the eye-popping potential of flight. In 1920, people viewed airplanes as entertainment; they flocked to air fields near circuses and country fairs to be thrilled as stunt pilots or "barnstormers" performed loop-the-loops in former army planes. Many saw the airplane's only practical peacetime function as a fast means of mail delivery. Then in 1925, Congress passed the Kelly Act to help the air carrier industry provide facilities for transporting passengers. Still, airplanes, most of which held only eight to twelve travelers, did not attract many passengers because they were uncomfortable, noisy, and perceived as dangerous. The airplane industry would provide no more than 2.3 percent of the total passenger transport market during the next fifteen years.

❖ CONSTRUCTION AND BUILDING

During the 1920s, there was a building boom in cities and suburbs across the nation. In 1925, total annual construction spending reached more than $6 billion, compared to slightly more than $919 million in 1916. In cities, commercial construction of hotels, office buildings, and apartment buildings reflected a growing economy. Many of these were multistory, art deco-designed buildings. In the suburbs, residential tract housing was springing up to meet the growing demand for homes located in the peace and beauty of the countryside, but within an automobile's reach of jobs. Specialized banks, later known as savings-and-loan institutions, offered long-term mortgages to home buyers at affordable rates; these lending groups also allowed their members to pay for automobiles in installments. Residential houses usually sold for $3,500 to $5,000, but many blue-collar workers earned only $1,200 to $1,800 per year. So, while suburban life may have appealed to many Americans, it was affordable only to those in the middle class that held secure jobs. As residential housing grew in the suburbs, so did the need to build suburban schools, civic buildings, and shopping areas. At the same time, middle-class suburbanites with expendable incomes called for the construction of recreational country clubs and golf courses.

Meanwhile, wealthy industrialists were paying for the construction of two very different types of buildings: academic structures and industrial plants. Through philanthropic foundations, multimillionaire families such as Rockefeller, Morgan, and Duke were funding the building of new libraries and classrooms at universities and colleges across the country, many of which were designed to mirror the intricate Western European Gothic structures of past centuries. The same private fortunes were paying to put up modern factories with improved electricity, better lighting and increased ventilation. Industrial architect Albert Kahn (1869–1942) designed a number of automobile plants for Henry Ford (1863–1947) during the decade, including the Ford Motor Company's tremendous River Rouge plant, which opened just in time to start production of the new Model A automobile in 1927.

The building boom came to an abrupt halt in late 1929 when the stock market crashed. Many huge commercial projects, such as the Empire State Building in Manhattan, built from 1929 to 1931, remained almost vacant until the next real estate boom in 1941, when the United States entered World War II.

❖ AGRICULTURAL PRODUCTION

Farmers did not take part in the prosperity of the 1920s. The industry was made up of thousands of small farmers, none of whom had control over the marketplace. Additionally, the make-up of American farming did not lend itself to benefit from the same advantages other industries enjoyed. Farming is dependent upon natural forces such as weather, and in spite of all the modern technologies that were being applied to farm production in the 1920s, such as trucks, tractors, electricity, and chemical fertilizers, there was an ongoing problem of overused farmland. Because one farm's output pretty much duplicated the neighboring farm's, the agriculture industry could not attract buyers based on competitive advertising. After all, wheat is wheat! Farming as a lifestyle was considered rather dull to a young rural generation who left their parents' farms for the cities seeking better-paying jobs and jazz-age adventure.

Even so, certain types of farm production did increase during the 1920s. Citrus growers in Florida and California prospered as the demand for oranges and grapefruits rose. Livestock producers thrived as the well-heeled consumer's demand for meat increased. In general, however, farmers suffered, particularly the southern cotton growers and the midwestern grain growers. While the government was busy supporting industry, neither the administration of Warren Harding (1865–1923) nor Calvin Coolidge (1872–1933) showed much interest in the plight of the American farmer. In fact, Coolidge vetoed the McNary-Haugen Bill which promised relief for farmers.

❖ GOVERNMENT AND BUSINESS

Whereas the administration of Woodrow Wilson (1856–1924) took an active part in regulating big business, the policies of Warren Harding and Calvin Coolidge emphasized a "laissez-faire" attitude, drastically cutting governmental control of industry. Except for the regulation of the railroads, public utilities, radio broadcasting, and air carriers, the federal government rarely involved itself with industry. Harding's so-called "rule of reason" worked to counter the existing antitrust laws (legislation which keeps businesses from illegally restraining competition), and although a minimum wage for workers was set by the federal government, there were no government unemployment benefits, Social Security benefits, or other labor/consumer protections. Much of Wilson's reform program, known as the "New Freedom," went by the wayside with the advent of World War I. The 1920s was a decade of temporary prosperity due in part to low taxes and the encouragement of the growth of big business.

Harding was concerned mainly with a quick return to prewar "normalcy," and he was so anxious to remove wartime restraints from American life that he took shortcuts that later resulted in charges of corruption and scandal. Coolidge was more careful in fulfilling his presidential duties, but his belief in a frugal government with a small national budget allowed business to prosper without federal intervention. When Coolidge was warned that the stock market was starting to spin out of control, he was concerned at first. However, when he later learned that the New York Stock Exchange's collapse fell under the jurisdiction of the state of New York and not the federal government, Coolidge was relieved because he would not have to take corrective action.

Aside from the aircraft industry, the only other business in which the government took an active part during the 1920s was the radio industry. By the middle of the decade, there were so many commercial radio stations that a predicament arose over the frequencies at which they broadcast. The stations with the strongest frequencies were attracting the most listeners. While the radio audience delighted in receiving long-distance stations, local advertisers were fuming because the listener, and potential customer, who lived one mile down the road was picking up the signal of a station one hundred miles away. To alleviate this problem, President Coolidge signed legislation to create a regulatory body within the Commerce Department that later became the Federal Communications Commission (FCC). This body regulated the frequencies at which radio stations were allowed to operate.

❖ THE AIRCRAFT INDUSTRY

Following the Kelly Act of 1920, the government began to subsidize aircraft companies that produced airplanes to carry mail. One pioneer contractor in the aircraft industry was Seattle-based lumber businessman William Boeing (1881–1956), who in 1925 won a contract to deliver mail between San Francisco and Chicago without having a plane that could do the job! To fulfill his contract, Boeing produced the 40A model aircraft which could carry 1,200 pounds of mail, and later a few passengers, over the Sierra Nevada and the Rocky Mountains. The 40A, which had been designed by expert engineers, sold for $25,000 and attracted many buyers. This success marked the beginning of Boeing Aircraft, the largest airplane manufacturer in the world.

By mid-decade, the fledgling but well-organized aircraft industry included the group of corporate contractors who would dominate the industry up to the start of World War II. Among them were Boeing, Ryan, Glenn L. Martin, Douglas Aircraft, Lockheed, Curtiss-Wright, and even the Ford Motor Company, which was manufacturing the tri-motor airplane (nicknamed the Tin Goose).

❖ THE AUTOMOBILE INDUSTRY

In 1920, the best-selling car on the road was the Ford Motor Company's Model T, which at its lowest price cost $260. Ford had sold 17 million of these cars. Between 1900 and 1930, more than two thousand car manufacturers had been in business. Smaller firms such as Packard, Nash, Hudson, Franklin, Duesenberg, and Pierce-Arrow generally made high-priced, high quality automobiles. Despite the existence of so many companies, the public bought cars mainly from the "Big Three": General Motors (GM), Chrysler, and Ford. GM provided the Chevrolet, Chrysler the Plymouth, and Ford the Model T and Model A.

The Day the New Cars Arrived in Town

The day that new car models arrived at local dealerships across America was a very special day indeed. Each year, during September and October, the next-year-model Fords, Chevrolets, and Plymouths, as well as the higher-priced Lincolns, Packards, and Cadillacs, would be transported by special railroad cars to communities across the country. The cars would be unpacked at the freight yards and driven to well-lit showrooms in dealerships. Potential customers and "window shoppers" alike flocked to see the cars and pick up brochures that described the advantages of the new intriguing updates, such as hydraulic brakes, "free wheeling," "the turret top," "knee action," and "synchro-mesh transmission."

The popularity of cars brought about economic growth not only in automobile manufacturing, but also in related businesses such as car dealerships, auto parts and supplies manufacturers, petroleum-product developers, and service stations and garages. The number of businesses actually influenced by the increased use of the automobile is a long one: cars brought about the construction of highways and roads linking major cities and small communities all across the country; cars resulted in the rise of the suburbs; car travel produced enterprises such as tourist-court motels, some known as "motor inns," and motorist amenities such as gasoline stations and roadside restaurants.

For the first quarter of the twentieth century, owning any car was a status symbol. Later, owning a *new* car model became the goal of most Americans. By the late 1920s, car manufacturers landed upon the idea of making changes in car models each year to keep their sales up. By that time, the automobile industry was the largest in the United States. In 1926, 4.2 million cars were manufactured, and by 1930 that figure had risen to 5.3 million. It has been estimated that Americans owned 39 percent of the world's production of automobiles by 1927, when GM and Ford cars also were popular in Europe.

❖ RADIO AND BROADCASTING

The use of radio was limited to hobbyists and communications specialists in its early days. In 1920, KDKA became the first commercial radio station. Other stations quickly followed. In those days, an investor with

Radio Programming

Radios began to be marketed for home use in 1920 and more than five million were sold each year of the decade. In 1925, more than 70 percent of broadcast time was devoted to music. Only 1 percent was dedicated to drama; 7 percent to news, and 2 percent to sports. Each week, radio stations also broadcast speeches from civic and professional organizations.

just $20,000 could set up and run a radio station, although a fallback fund was necessary to pay for maintaining the specialized technical equipment. In the 1910s, stations mainly broadcast news or general information; soon, however, it became apparent to radio industry pioneers such as David Sarnoff (1891–1971), a New York City-based telegraph operator who eventually molded the modern communications industry through Radio Corporation of America (RCA), that radio could be used as a profitable means of entertainment with commercial sponsorship in the form of on-air advertisements. Between 1921 and 1929, the value of radios owned in the country rose from $10.6 million to $411 million.

Radios in homes reached the ears of two thousand Americans in 1920; there were 2.5 million radio listeners by the beginning of 1924. As radio became a major pastime of the American public, the government set up a bureau within the Department of Commerce to regulate broadcasting. Two major functions of the bureau were to keep stations from trespassing on each other's frequencies and to coordinate overlapping programs such as national political addresses.

❖ THE GROWTH OF RETAIL

Middle-class and working-class Americans prospered during the 1920s, which led directly to a growth in retail trade. With the spread of residential areas to the suburbs, retailers found new locations to do business. Many merchants decided to open multiple stores in various neighborhoods, giving rise to the concept of the retail chain. By 1927, some fifteen hundred retail companies were operating stores in nearly seventy thousand locations; popular chains included the A&P and Kroger food stores, J.C. Penney department stores, Walgreen drugstores, Fanny Farmer candy stores, and Child's restaurants. Certain chain stores offered employees the opportunity to buy stock in the company and gave young managers the chance to rise through the ranks to corporate positions. Retail management had come a long way from such outdated nineteenth-century marketing practices as drummers (salesmen) leading horses and wagons from town to town. Now, university graduates were formulating scientific marketing methods and relying upon modern advertising campaigns to motivate American consumers to spend their money on all sorts of products.

The rise of chain stores provoked strong competition among the large mail-order companies that had arisen at the end of the nineteenth century, including Sears Roebuck and Montgomery Ward. In the meantime, the department stores in big cities became even grander in their structures and extravagant in their choice of merchandise. In New York City, Saks Fifth Avenue sold raccoon coats for $1,000 each, pigskin trunks for $3,000, and even livery (uniforms) for the family chauffeur! Through merger and consolidation (buying and/or combining with other companies), retail firms became big-city selling powerhouses. For instance, Gimbel Brothers in New York City acquired Kaufman's in Pittsburgh, and similarly, in 1929 Lazarus Brothers took over Abraham & Straus in New York City, Filene's in Boston, Bullock's in California, and other chain department stores to create Federated Department Stores.

❖ LAND SPECULATION AND THE FLORIDA BOOM

Before the 1920s, Florida was a relatively undeveloped state; there was very little industry except for some tourism and agriculture. One of the first promoters of the Florida land boom was an outsider to the state, millionaire Henry M. Flagler (1830–1913) of Standard Oil. In the 1890s, Flagler put through the Florida East Coast Railroad, and then saw fit to build a number of luxury hotels and resorts. A major publicity campaign was waged to attract Americans to purchase thousands of low-cost lots in the warm climate of snowless winters and exotic terrain. Throughout the early 1920s, land speculators were buying lots for immediate resale at tremendous profits. This pattern escalated as the land was subdivided again and again for resale at substantial profit.

The boom slowed in 1925 when northern newspapers cautioned the public about the dangers of spending such inflated amounts of money on strips of poorly developed land. Then on September 18, 1926, a powerful hurricane swept through the east coast of Florida, killing hundreds and obliterating the many cheaply constructed homes that had been built by eager investors. In some ways, the Florida land boom crash foreshadowed the stock market crash of 1929.

❖ THE STOCK MARKET BOOM GOES BUST

Commercial banks expanded their activities during the 1920s. Financial institutions such as the Bank of America and Chase Manhattan Bank grew more powerful through mergers and consolidation and used their combined resources for construction and consumer loans. Investment banks (banks which did little or no commercial business such as handling checking accounts, but instead lent money to entrepreneurs) became more plentiful; there were 277 investment banks in 1912, but their number rose to 1,902 by 1929.

Wall Street investing had always been thought of as a pastime for the wealthy; by 1920, however, the middle class began to invest in the stock market. Ever since they had bought Liberty Bonds during World War I, Americans had felt more open to buying stocks in an increasing number of public corporations. Stockbrokers began opening offices in cities across the country to accommodate the investing public. It became quite stylish to invest in the stock market, and casual conversation often included the latest stock tips. In general, it was safe to invest funds in the market, because firms such as American Telephone & Telegraph, General Motors, Radio Corporation of America, and U.S. Steel were expanding rapidly and making increased profits for investors. When Charles Lindbergh (1902–1974) successfully flew the first solo nonstop transatlantic flight in 1927, investors became enthusiastic about airplane and aircraft-related stocks.

Stock trading volume rose steadily until the summer of 1929, when Wall Street brokers could not keep up with the mounting paperwork. The

Wall Street Industrial Averages for October 1929

Date	Last Average	Net Change	Day's Sales
1	431.13	-4.06	4,524,810
2	434.66	+3.53	3,367,610
3	415.14	-19.52	4,747,330
4	408.64	-6.50	5,634,900
5	424.96	+16.32	2,451,870
6	Sunday		
7	432.85	+7.89	4,261,900
8	437.43	+4.66	3,758,090
9	439.84	+2.39	3,156,740
10	446.49	+6.63	3,999,730
11	443.07	-1.42	3,963,820
12	Holiday		
13	Sunday		
14	442.77	-2.30	2,755,850
15	440.83	-1.94	3,107,050
16	427.73	-13.10	4,088,000
17	434.56	+6.83	3,864,150
18	427.36	-7.20	3,507,740
19	415.18	-12.18	3,488,100
20	Sunday		
21	409.23	-5.95	6,091,870
22	415.07	+5.84	4,129,820
23	384.10	-30.97	6,374,960
24	371.91	-12.19	12,894,650
25	372.66	+0.75	5,923,220
26	367.42	-5.25	2,087,660
27	Sunday		
28	318.29	-49.12	9,212,800
29	275.26	-43.03	16,410,030
30	306.21	+30.95	10,727,320
31	327.12	+20.91	7,149,390

Source: *New York Times* October 1–31, 1929.

number of shares of stocks sold was rising to unimagined heights. For example, on September 3, 4.4 million shares were sold. What made the situation dangerous was the fact that investors were buying on margin (credit), a situation that was tolerable only while the market was rising. Many experts cautioned the public about the vulnerability of the stock

*Crowds moving past the
New York Stock Exchange
building on October 29,
1929, the day the market
crashed. This date also
became known as "Black
Tuesday" and marked the
beginning of the Great
Depression.* **Reproduced by
permission of AP/Wide
World Photos.**

market, but most investors were so enthusiastic about the profits they
were making that they refused to listen to warnings.

Traders who bought stocks on margin paid a portion of the price of
the stock and then relied on future profit in order to complete payment of
the transaction. If the stock fell, the customer would have to put in more
money to sustain the account. In September 1929, stockbrokers' loans
totaled $670 million—a good sign that signaled continued interest in the
market, but also a bad sign that displayed the weak "house of cards" that
market transactions had become. If a stock were to fall and then keep
falling, the investor could not pay money owed to the broker; and the broker, in turn, could not pay the loan to the New York banks which had bor-
rowed from the Federal Reserve, the leaders of the nation's financial system. Also, because paperwork methods were primitive and usually days
behind transactions and the tickertape (the ribbon on which a telegraphic
machine prints information) announcing current stock prices usually was
one hour behind, investors would not be able to keep up with market
action if a crisis occurred.

During the 1920s, primitive methods of announcing stock prices, like this tickertape machine, did not allow investors to keep up with market action. **Reproduced by permission of the Corbis Corporation.**

That crisis came on October 24, 1929. First, communications failed as the ticker lagged and the telephone lines became jammed, leaving investors ignorant of a tremendous amount of trading action in the market. Before the morning ended, brokers were selling huge blocks of stock for whatever price they would bring. As the selling continued, the decorum of the stock

The show business trade
paper Variety *displaying
the now legendary
headline: "Wall St. Lays
an Egg," referring to the
Stock Market Crash of
1929. Reproduced by
permission of the
Corbis Corporation.*

market floor had slid from dignified quiet into loud shouting, and the public gallery was closed by the acting president of the New York Stock
Exchange, Richard Whitney (1888–1974). Whitney called a meeting of top
Wall Street bankers and then, in a brash move to bolster trader confidence
when everyone else was selling out, he purchased a purported $20 million

worth of blue-chip stocks (stocks from well-established companies that normally hold great value). His action was witnessed by all those on the stock exchange floor. This bold move temporarily calmed investors, but the system fell apart altogether on the following "Black Tuesday," October 29, 1929, when traders sold stocks in huge quantities until the market completely caved in to the frailties of the system. Many who were buying stocks on margin lost their fortunes and went deeply into debt. Brokers lost their businesses, and banks could not recover their loans.

The stock market crash pushed the U.S. economy from the prosperity of the 1920s to the eventual Great Depression of the 1930s. Never again would the government remain so uninvolved as to allow citizens to play haphazardly in the market. Bankers who had been among the most respectable members of the community were now seen as questionable characters. Many of them were brought before congressional committees and charged with mismanagement. Some were even criminally prosecuted. Although not every investor lost money, many lifestyles were radically changed and some investors with heavy losses committed suicide. The show business trade paper *Variety* summed up the desperate situation with the now legendary headline: "Wall St. Lays an Egg."

For More Information

BOOKS

Allen, Frederick Lewis. *America Transforms Itself: 1900–1950*. New Brunswick, NJ: Transaction Pub., 1993 (reprint edition).

Brennan, Kristine. *The Stock Market Crash of 1929*. Philadelphia: Chelsea House, 2000.

Chant, Christopher. *Famous Trains of the 20th Century*. Philadelphia: Chelsea House, 2000.

Feinberg, Barbara Silberdick. *Black Tuesday: The Stock Market Crash of 1929*. Brookfield, CT: Millbrook Press, 1995.

Galbraith, John Kenneth. *The Great Crash: 1929*. Boston: Houghton Mifflin, 1997 (reprint edition).

Gay, Kathlyn. *Who's Running the Nation? How Corporate Power Threatens Democracy*. New York: Franklin Watts, 1998.

Hanson, Erica. *The 1920s*. San Diego, CA: Lucent Books, 1999.

Katz, William Loren. *The New Freedom to the New Deal, 1913–1939*. Austin, TX: Raintree Steck-Vaughn, 1993.

Meltzer, Milton. *Brother, Can You Spare a Dime?: The Great Depression, 1929–1933*. New York, Facts on File, 1991 (reprint edition).

O'Connell, Arthur J. *American Business in the 20th Century.* San Mateo, CA: Blue-wood Books, 1999.

Sherrow, Victoria. *Hardship and Hope: America and the Great Depression.* New York: Twenty-First Century Books, 1997.

Stewart, Gail. *1910s.* New York: Crestwood House, 1989.

WEB SITES

The First Measured Century: Timeline Events—Stock Market Crash. http://www.pbs.org/fmc/timeline/estockmktcrash.htm (accessed on August 2, 2002).

1920s. http://www.richland2.org/svh/Media/socstud/1920s.htm (accessed on August 5, 2002).

The 1920s: Business and Industry Trends and Leaders of the Roaring Twenties. http://www.louisville.edu/~kprayb01/1920s-Business.html (accessed on August 2, 2002).

Education

1920: The U.S. Census states that 21,578,000 students are enrolled in public schools. Colleges have 597,000 students.

1920: The Dalton Plan of instruction is first utilized by educators in Dalton, Massachusetts. The Plan is a progressive approach to education that tailors learning to individual students' needs and talents.

1920: The Lusk Laws are passed, making it necessary for teachers in the state of New York to sign loyalty oaths.

1920: Susan Miller Dorsey becomes the country's first woman superintendent of schools. She is appointed superintendent of the Los Angeles public school system.

1920: Ellwood P. Cubberley of Stanford University publishes *The History of Education.*

1920: December 4–10 American Education Week is first celebrated.

1921: Approximately two hundred universities are awarding master's degrees, and nearly fifty offer doctorate degrees.

1921: January 18 The New York state school commissioner declares that public school teachers who hold active memberships in the Communist Party are subject to dismissal.

1922: *The Selective Character of American Secondary Education* by George S. Counts is published.

1922: *Human Nature and Conduct* by John Dewey draws a large readership.

1923: The Supreme Court rules in *Meyer* v. *Nebraska* that it is unconstitutional to ban the instruction of foreign languages.

1923: Winter The Lusk Laws are repealed.

1923: October 16 The New York Court of Appeals sustains a law which requires educational and literacy tests for new voters.

1924: William McAndrew is appointed superintendent of the Chicago public school system.

1924: March 31 An Oregon law which requires all children to attend public schools is ruled unconstitutional by the U.S. Supreme Court.

1924: May 21 The General Assembly of the Presbyterian Church in San Antonio, Texas, rules that the teaching of the

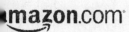

SDxjTNhBhh

Item	Item Price	Total
Panasonic FV-0511VKL2 WhisperGreen Multi-Flow Bathroom Fan, White Tools & Home Improvement X001Z4Z0AL SD-PAN-0098 885170337299 **(Sold by Teak Products)**	$259.99	$259.99

shipment completes your order.

	Subtotal	$259.99
	Tax Collected	$16.25
	Order Total	$276.24
	Paid via credit/debit	$276.24

rn or replace your item
Ama   eturns

TNh6nh, 1 of 1–//KRFD-KIA   c/0/1017-03:00/1016-20.54   **PA**

theory of evolution in public schools is insupportable.

1925: Author and editor Glenn Frank becomes president of the University of Wisconsin, where he enacts education reforms.

1925: May 13 The Florida State House of Representatives passes a bill requiring daily Bible readings in all public schools.

1925: July 10 John T. Scopes goes on trial for teaching the theory of evolution to his students in Dayton, Tennessee.

1925: October 16 The Texas State Text Book Board bans books that discuss the theory of evolution.

1925: December 29 The trustees of Trinity College in North Carolina agree to change the name of their school to Duke University, in honor of tobacco industrialist James B. Duke, who donated $40 million to the school.

1926: Carter Godwin Woodson is awarded the Spingarn Medal by the National Association for the Advancement of Colored People (NAACP), for promoting the study of African American history.

1926: Julian Butterworth publishes *Principles of Rural School Administration.*

1926: A test case enters the court system requiring the White Plains, New York school board to grant one hour of religious instruction for school children.

1926: February 9 The board of education of Atlanta, Georgia, bans the teaching of the theory of evolution in the public schools.

1927: New York University sets up seven summer schools within European universities. College credit will be granted if the courses are taught by American professors.

1927: Glenn Frank recruits Alexander Meiklejohn, author of a number of influential books on education, to establish and run the Experimental College at the University of Wisconsin.

1928: George S. Counts publishes the revealing account *School and Society in Chicago.*

1929: The Carnegie Foundation for the Advancement of Teaching reports that collegiate athletics have become a "Roman Circus."

1929: Public school enrollment is 25,678,000, and enrollment in colleges and universities is more than 1,000,000.

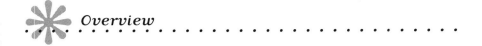

Overview

Following a trend towards progressive education which began earlier in the twentieth century, reforms continued in school curricula, teacher training, and styles of instruction during the 1920s. In accordance with the progressive education movement (which focused on educating the whole person instead of enforcing the memorization of key facts), educators conducted laboratory studies, tracked educational statistics, and published the results of their findings. The resulting body of work described the habits and performance of the American student. These studies were analyzed and used to enact further reforms in educational psychology and philosophy.

Meanwhile, with the return of American troops at the end of World War I in 1918, many new babies were born. That population increase led to larger elementary school enrollments in the 1920s. The number of students enrolled in secondary schools and institutions of higher learning also rose dramatically. All this expansion caused a building boom in public school districts. Adding to the increased enrollments in secondary schools was the nation's added awareness of the role that public education played in helping young adults find suitable jobs. Throughout the decade, more vocational programs were set up in public schools. Those programs drew support from businesses and corporations willing to sponsor potential workers of the near future. At the same time, a huge population of immigrants had settled in the United States. The need to educate those new Americans in language, literacy, customs, and citizenship sparked a nationally organized movement to establish evening classes in many schools.

As more Americans acquired secondary education, a good number decided to continue learning in degree programs at colleges and universities. Educators made strides to enact reforms on campuses to create curricula of academic interest and practical use to the many Americans who were entering business, agriculture, or service careers such as teaching.

Colleges and universities were being expanded and reorganized to meet the needs of modern society in the 1920s. Among the programs to be rethought and expanded were sports and athletics. In the 1920s, higher learning extended to the playing fields, where football, baseball, swimming, and golf became popular team sports. Since the economy was prospering, many families now had the assets to send the younger generation to college. Furthermore, once a student graduated, a variety of suitable jobs were available, making the choice to pursue higher education an economically sound decision.

Public school systems were supported mainly through state and local taxes. That situation resulted in inequality among school districts. Those who lived and went to school in upscale cities and wealthy suburbs had more books, better buildings and equipment, and teachers who were higher paid and often better trained. Those pupils in poor rural areas had to make do with what little their school districts could put together. Standardization in schools through federal bureaucracy and government legislation was still in its infancy.

Lingering fears from World War I also had their effect on American education. Following the "Red Scare" of 1919 and 1920, some Americans feared communist infiltration of the school systems. In certain public schools and on college and university campuses, the administration required teachers to sign oaths stating that they were loyal Americans and not communists. At institutions of higher learning, professors with unconventional ideas sometimes were distrusted to the point of being dismissed. As the decade progressed, however, these demands for compliance were deemed unconstitutional. As these restraints were reversed, school administrators still concerned themselves with arguments surrounding free speech and academic freedoms. One of the most fiery debates of the decade centered on the instruction of the theory of evolution in schools. This controversy affected the school curricula in a number of states, and resulted in one of the most highly publicized trials of the early twentieth century: the Scopes Monkey Trial of 1925.

Mary McLeod Bethune (1875–1955) In 1904, African American educator Mary McLeod Bethune founded the Daytona Normal and Industrial Institute for Negro Girls in Daytona Beach, Florida. In 1923, that institution merged with the Cookman Institute for Men to become Bethune-Cookman College. Bethune was active in the women's rights movement and organized the National Council of Negro Women in the early 1930s. Her involvement with national conferences on education, child welfare, and home ownership brought her to the attention of the nation's first lady, Eleanor Roosevelt (1884–1962), during the New Deal reform era of the 1930s. Their relationship led Bethune to serve as director of Negro affairs in the National Youth Administration (1936–44). She also advised President Franklin Roosevelt (1882–1945) on matters involving minorities.

Photo reproduced by permission of the Estate of Carl Van Vechten.

Nicholas Murray Butler (1862–1947) As a philosophy professor (1885–1901) at Columbia College in New York City, Nicholas Murray Butler designed plans to expand and modernize the college. He founded the Teachers' College at Columbia in 1889 and became its first president. Butler helped structure a plan by which Columbia College was turned into Columbia University. It was Butler who brought influential, progressive educators John Dewey, William Heard Kilpatrick, and George S. Counts to the Teachers' College. Butler's involvements ranged from teacher training to world politics. He was awarded the Nobel Peace Prize in 1931 for his work on the Pact of Paris, and he founded the Carnegie Endowment for International Peace, serving as its president from 1925 to 1945. *Photo reproduced by permission of Archive Photos, Inc.*

Alvin Saunders Johnson (1874–1971) Alvin Saunders Johnson cofounded the New School for Social Research in 1919, and held the position of director from 1923 to 1945. Under his guidance, the New York City-based school became a preeminent institution of adult learning. In 1933, Johnson set up the "University in Exile" as a refuge for European scholars who had escaped from the Nazis. With the help of the Rockefeller Foundation, he arranged for more than two hundred expatriate scholars to study in the United States. Johnson also was an editor of the *New Republic* and the *Encyclopedia of the Social Sciences.*

William Heard Kilpatrick (1871–1965) A disciple of leading progressive education theorist John Dewey (1859–1952), William Heard Kilpatrick brought the theories and philosophies of progressive education to a more radical level than his mentor. As a principal in several Georgia public school systems in the 1890s, Kilpatrick abolished report cards and student punishments. His style of teaching downplayed the instructor as the center of attention and focused classroom activity on student discussion. An eloquent speaker, Kilpatrick became known as "The Million-Dollar Professor" after his classes' enrollment fees of a single summer topped that amount. *Photo reproduced courtesy of the Library of Congress.*

Abbott Lawrence Lowell (1855–1943) During his tenure as president of Harvard University (1909–33), Abbott Lawrence Lowell revamped the style of learning by emphasizing the significance of an academic community on campus, and redesigning the student housing system into freshmen dormitories and residential colleges. His defense of academic freedom attracted some of the world's top professors to Harvard. It had been his intention to use his Harvard Law School degree to pursue a partnership in a Boston law firm with other family members, and then become a judge. Instead, he dedicated his career to education and the study of government. *Photo reproduced courtesy of the Library of Congress.*

Topics in the News

❖ EDUCATION OF THE IMMIGRANT POPULATION

Overcoming the problem of illiteracy (the inability to read and write) was a fundamental challenge for educators who participated in a national movement in the late 1910s to assimilate (absorb into the American culture) the newly arrived foreign born. At the start of the 1920s, almost five million illiterate people over the age of ten were living in America. As more immigrants settled in the United States, the rate of illiteracy grew to be as high as 25 to 35 percent.

Among the groups who took on the responsibility of immigrant education were the Federal Bureau of Education and the naturalization division of the U.S. Immigration and Naturalization Service. The organizations published a textbook on citizenship training, which was distributed to all accredited schools at no cost. In 1921, the National Education Association (NEA) set up the Department of Immigration Education to teach American culture to immigrants. Labor groups, churches and synagogues, and local civic organizations sponsored classes in the English language, American history, civics, and industrial education.

Recognizing the diversity in society, educators began to institute changes in the character, purpose, and direction of American education. In the 1920s, literacy and citizenship became focal points in American public school education. Not just for immigrants, but for all the population, education was considered a worthy expenditure of tax dollars. Many people believed that education led to a better and more meaningful quality of life, and even to a more virtuous way of life.

❖ EDUCATION AND POLITICS

Senator Clayton R. Lusk (1872–1959), chairman of the New York state legislative committee investigating sedition (actions challenging the authority of the government), pushed for the enactment of "Loyalty Laws" in 1920 and 1921. These laws required public school teachers to obtain certificates of loyalty and character from the state commissioner of education. Many teachers were opposed to this process, believing it to be a breach of their civil liberties; in 1923, under the guidance of Governor Alfred E. Smith (1873–1944), the Lusk laws were repealed.

Anti-German sentiments were so strong during World War I that state education administrators were motivated to make changes in curricula. Eleven states enacted laws to forbid the teaching of foreign languages in private and public schools. Learning to speak German, in particular, was considered akin to adopting a dangerous political and cultural influence. In 1923, however, the Supreme Court ruled in *Meyer* v. *Nebraska* that laws banning the instruction of foreign languages were unconstitutional.

The state of Oregon passed a law in 1922 requiring all children to attend public schools. The legislation was aimed at closing parochial schools and other types of private schools that did not adhere to the Protestant ethic. In the 1924 case of *Pierce* v. *Society of Sisters of the Holy Names*, the Supreme Court decided that the Oregon statute was unconstitutional because it did not give parents the right to choose schools for their children.

Because so much of public education was funded through local taxes, it was inevitable that corrupt politicians occasionally misused funds stipulated for public school systems. In Chicago in the early 1920s, Mayor William Hale "Big Bill" Thompson (1869–1944) and his corrupt "political machine" illegally obstructed the work of the board of education, raided monies set aside for education, and dipped into the teachers' pension fund. Then in 1923, Thompson was "dethroned" and a more honest mayoral candidate was elected. The new mayor appointed William McAndrew (1863–1926) as superintendent of schools, and McAndrew proceeded to enact a series of reforms. Unfortunately, Chicago politics dissolved into a war of opposing factions, with McAndrew's reforms at the center of much debate. In the scuffle, the dishonest group regained control. In 1927, Thompson was re-elected mayor. McAndrew was ousted, and his reforms were reversed. During the 1920s, this type of problem plagued communities across the country. In his publication *School and Society in Chicago* (1928), noted scholar George S. Counts (1889–1974) brought the public's attention to the dangers of mixing questionable politics with education. As an example, Counts bravely cited the situation in Chicago.

❖ PROGRESS THROUGH CURRICULUM CHANGES

In 1925, Professor Ellwood P. Cubberley (1886–1965) of Stanford University advocated an introductory course in education to be required of prospective teachers in all colleges, universities, and normal schools (two-year teacher-training schools). He did so to counter the growing specialization within education departments. Cubberley was concerned that students who took a very specific education course, or even several of the narrowly defined courses, would graduate without having acquired an overview or general philosophy of education and teaching methods.

Throughout the decade, teacher training grew more detailed and more challenging. The two-year normal school programs were being superseded by

John Dewey on Teaching

As a people, we profess to believe in education above everything else. We have succeeded in making ourselves believe in this profession. Critics are taken in by it, and ridicule our alleged faith as a blind religion and our devotion to schools as a cult, a superstitious mummery. But what is the test of the depth and sincerity of a faith? Only acts show whether a professed belief is living or is a form of words. In the case of education the actions which serve as a test are: First, are we willing to pay, to give, to sacrifice, to get and keep in our elementary schools the kind of men and women teachers who alone can make our schools be what they should be? And, secondly, apart from money for salaries and equipment of schools for educational work, what are we willing to do in the way of esteem, respect, social prestige, hearty backing? For neither question is the answer very encouraging, least of all for elementary schools.

Immediately after the war the shortage of teachers was such as to compel some attention to the question of adjustment of wages in the face of the rise in the cost of living. The Red Scare helped also, as least as far as high school and college teachers were concerned, since there was a fear that poorly paid 'intellectuals' would be attracted toward Bolshevism [a form of Russian communism, circa 1917, which advocated the violent fall of capitalism]. But symptoms only, not causes, were then dealt with, and that remains true today. Salaries were increased in reference to quantity and not quality. The aim was simply to pay what was demanded in order to get enough teachers to go around, such as they were; not to find out what would be required to attract and hold the best men and women within the schools.

Source: Jo Ann Boydston, ed. "What is the Matter with Teaching," in *John Dewey: The Later Works, 1925–1953*, volume 2, 1925–27, (Carbondale & Edwardsville: Southern Illinois University Press, 1984) p. 117.

four-year programs. New approaches to education were being considered, such as those that were based on the relationship between child development and educational philosophy. In addition to the many students in education programs, certified teachers also were seeking more knowledge about their work. They flocked to lecture halls and signed up for summer training sessions to hear the ideas of Cubberley, along with progressive education champions John Dewey (1859–1952) and William Heard Kilpatrick (1871–1965) of Columbia

University. From their early-century role as taskmaster, modern teachers were evolving into more complex, creative, and nurturing professionals.

Since the 1910s, the broadening recognition of the value of a progressive education was having a positive effect on curricula. Across the country, school systems gradually were branching out from the old-fashioned rote learning of the "three Rs"—reading, 'riting, and 'rithmetic—to a broader range of topics: algebra, geometry, civics, American government and history, as well as industrial arts, home economics, and personal hygiene. Progressive educators felt that part of the learning process was to gain the interest of the student. They believed education prepared a student to be a good citizen as well as a productive member of the workforce.

The wide acceptance of the Dalton Laboratory Plan, or the Dalton Plan, was an indication of the growth of progressive education during the 1920s. Combining the theories of Dewey with those of Italian psychiatrist and educator Maria Montessori (1870–1952), whose work involved giving young children appropriate tools for them to learn by themselves, an experimental laboratory was established at a high school in Dalton, Massachusetts, during the 1920s. There, students worked on long-term projects. They researched topics, wrote papers, and gave oral presentations about their work. The Dalton Plan became a popular teaching approach in schools in the United States and Western Europe. A modified version of the plan was developed at the University of Wisconsin, in which the student and teacher began each project by drawing up a contract listing the grade the student wanted and the work required to achieve that grade. The Contract Plan, as it was called, also became a popular method of teaching during the 1920s.

❖ DEMOGRAPHIC CHANGES

After World War I, there was a boom in baby births. As the 1920s began, there were thirteen million preschool-aged children in the United States. Twenty-five million children were between the ages of ten and fifteen, and another ten million were between sixteen and twenty. The decade also saw a recognition of the critical need for compulsory elementary schooling, and the understanding of the importance of secondary education to help prepare young Americans to find a suitable place in their country's growing economy. Consideration of these realities led school administrators to construct new buildings and hire many more teachers. As a result, nearly eight thousand additional high schools were established during the decade, and nearly sixty thousand additional teachers were hired.

As early as 1910, the idea of the central schoolhouse for grades one through twelve was being phased out. By the early 1920s, the most preva-

Pupils in Public and Private High Schools: 1869 to 1930

Year	Number of Public High Schools	Students in Public and Private High Schools	% of Students in Public High Schools	% of Students in Private High Schools	% of Total Population
1869–70	c. 500	80,227			2.0
1879–80	c. 800	110,289			3.0
1889–90	2,526	202,969	68.13	31.87	5.0
1894–95	4,712	350,099	74.74	25.26	7.5
1899–1900	6,005	519,251	82.41	17.59	9.0
1904–05	7,576	679,702	86.38	13.62	10.0
1909–10	10,213	915,061	88.63	11.37	12.5
1914–15	11,674	1,328,984	89.55	10.45	20.0
1919–20	14,326	1,857,155	91.00	9.00	29.0
1924–25	c. 20,000	158,000	91.60	8.40	47.0
1929–30	c. 22,000				52.0

Note: Accurate comparable figures for recent years are not available due to the rise of the junior high school and the inclusion of data for these as part of the secondary school figures.

Source: Ellwood P. Cubberley, *Public Education in the United States* (Boston: Houghton Mifflin, 1934) p. 627.

lent plan for local school systems was the 6 to 3 to 3 division. Elementary school consisted of grades one through six; junior high school included grades seven through nine, and high school consisted of grades ten through twelve. As the teaching profession became more concerned with laboratory studies in educational psychology and philosophy, the three divisions offered a convenient means of gathering statistics by age group. For instance, studies relating to adolescent learning patterns would be conducted among junior high students.

High schools put the emphasis on preparing young adults for industry and society. There was a dramatic swell in the number of students who were attending high school. In fact, during the 1920s, a high school education reflected upon people's social class. Earning a high school graduation certificate meant an individual could move up from the lower working class into the highly skilled labor class.

❖ FUNDING FOR EDUCATION

Although a federal income tax was instituted in 1913, the amount of federal funding that trickled down to support public education was small. Public school systems relied heavily on state and local taxes. In 1924, only $4 million of school support came from the federal government, as compared to $262 million from the states, and over $1.3 billion from local sources. But in 1920, when Americans spent a total of $1 billion on candy, the total spent on education was nearly $1.04 billion!

Pleas for federal funding focused on gaining more money not only for instruction, but also to create equity for all school districts across the country. As long as state and local funding was the rule, public school systems in affluent regions of the country had better-quality schools than those in poor areas. During the decade, cities in New York State with a population of more than thirty thousand spent an average of 33 percent of their local budgets on education, while schools in rural areas of the state

Many southern schools were still one-room schoolhouses during the 1920s because of a lack of state and local funding. **Reproduced by permission of The Granger Collection.**

Annual Bill for Luxuries and School Expenditures for 1920

As the decade opened, very little money was being spent on education. What better way to illustrate this fact than to list the amounts Americans were spending on more "enjoyable" pastimes:

Candy	$1,000,000,000
Tobacco	$2,111,000,000
Soft drinks	$350,000,000
Perfume, cosmetics	$750,000,000
Theater admissions, dues, etc.	$800,000,000
Ice cream	$250,000,000
Cakes, confections	$350,000,000
Luxury foods	$5,000,000,000
Joy-riding, races, boxing and resorts	$3,000,000,000
Furs	$300,000,000
Carpets and luxury clothing	$1,500,000,000
Automobiles and Parts	$2,000,000,000
Toilet soaps	$400,000,000
Pianos and phonographs	$250,000,000
Total for Above Luxuries	$21,811,000,000
Total Spent on Education	$1,036,151,209

Source: Ellwood P. Cubberley, *An Introduction to the Study of Education and to Teaching* (Boston, Houghton Mifflin, 1925) p.444.

put aside an average of only 11 percent of their total budgets. This type of inequity also held true for the nation.

❖ THE SCOPES MONKEY TRIAL

During the 1920s, an ongoing controversy in schools was the teaching of human creation. Teachers who taught the scientifically accepted theories of evolution as the origin of human life came under the scrutiny of community members who favored the biblical account from the book of Genesis. This issue gained the attention of the world in March 1925 when a popular young teacher named John T. Scopes (1900–1970), employed in a small school district in Dayton, Tennessee, instructed his high school pupils in the scientific theories of creation. Scopes's instruction went against a new Tennessee law prohibiting the teaching of the evolution the-

ories of Charles Darwin (1809–1982) in state-funded schools. Tennessee was one of several southern states to have such a law on its books.

Darwin formulated his theories while he sailed around the world from 1831 to 1836 studying naturalism and geology. In his travels, Darwin noted the geographical distribution of plants and animals. He determined that species were capable of variations and that those in ecologically favorable environments could form new and distinct species. In 1859, Darwin published his seminal study *On The Origin of Species*. This publication led to passionate debate regarding the origin of the human race, especially by religious fundamentalists who placed the creation of humankind in the hands of a supernatural deity.

The leading citizens of Dayton invited two famous legal authorities, defense attorney Clarence Darrow (1857–1938) and prosecutor William Jennings Bryan (1860–1925), to argue the Scopes case, called the Scopes Monkey Trial by the media because Darwin's theories linked human evolution to that of apes. In an atmosphere of high tension and tremendous publicity, the two forceful personalities debated the case in July 1925. In the small courtroom the temperature often rose to 100 degrees. Eventually, Darrow was defeated, and Scopes was told to pay a fine of $100; however, a Tennessee appeals court overturned the ruling on a technicality. It was not until 1967 that Tennessee's evolution law was overturned by the Supreme Court.

❖ SPORTS IN EDUCATION

During the decade, colleges and universities began developing athletic programs and establishing intramural team sports (teams with players selected from among the student body who compete against one another and not against teams from other schools). Harvard and Yale set up intramural sports programs in the 1920s that included tennis, swimming, canoeing, golf, horseback riding, and badminton. Such activities were accepted as recreations among middle class and upper class society.

Physical education was added to the curricula of many colleges, and competition among school clubs was encouraged. During the decade, coaches started to teach in the classroom as well as on the athletic field. With more educated coach-teachers on faculty staffs, well thought-out physical education programs became ingrained in the upper-level American education system. Meanwhile, intercollegiate sports (contests between teams from different colleges) became so popular that in 1927, thirty million sports-minded fans paid a total of $50 million to attend college football games. In 1929 the Carnegie Report on Intercollegiate Athletics, published by the Carnegie Foundation for the Advancement of Teaching,

Martha Carey Thomas of Bryn Mawr

In 1922, Martha Carey Thomas (1857–1935) stepped down after serving as president of Bryn Mawr College since 1894. She had been a professor of English and later became the first woman in the United States to hold the title of dean. Additionally, Thomas helped establish the first graduate studies program at a women's college. She also was one of the founders of the International Federation of University Women and the Association to Promote Scientific Research. Thomas was a feminist and was active in the fight for women's suffrage (the right to vote).

expressed outrage at the commercialism of collegiate sports and labeled the excitement at the college stadiums a "Roman Circus." Indeed, collegiate football as well as other campus sports were taking on characteristics of professional sports and attracting big-time gambling. Even so, it would be many years before reforms were instituted to protect collegiate sports from unsavory elements.

❖ UNIVERSITY ENROLLMENTS

During the 1920s, as more young people began to graduate from high schools, college enrollments increased, particularly at state colleges and universities. At the University of California, the University of Georgia, and the University of Minnesota, enrollments tripled from 1915 to 1930. Private schools also gained many more students. University curricula developed programs that met the needs of a generation training to enter industry, agriculture, and the civil services, or to employ modern methods of home economics. College campuses were preparing a generation of teenagers and World War I veterans to meet the demands of the modern 1920s lifestyle.

Money was needed to allow colleges to expand and modernize curricula and facilities. Private donations increased dramatically, from $7.5 million in 1915 to $25 million in 1930. State and federal support rose from $62 million to $152 million. Of course, the stock market crash of October 1929 set the course of private donations into a downward plunge. Still, by the end of the decade 150,000 college and university degrees were being awarded each year, and the physical plant value of these institutions of higher learning totaled nearly $2 billion.

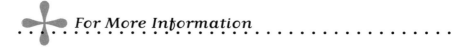

For More Information

BOOKS

Andryszewski, Tricia. *Immigration: Newcomers and Their Impact on the United States*. Brookfield, CT: Millbrook Press, 1995.

Andryszewski, Tricia. *School Prayer: A History of the Debate*. Springfield, NJ: Enslow Publishers, 1997.

Funk, Gary D. *A Balancing Act: Sports and Education*. Minneapolis: Lerner Publications Company, 1995.

Hanson, Freya Ottem. *The Scopes Monkey Trial: A Headline Court Case*. Berkeley Heights, NJ: Enslow Publishers, 2000.

Holt, Rackham. *Mary McLeod Bethune: A Biography*. Garden City, NY: Doubleday, 1964.

Lawrence, Jerome, and Robert E. Lee. *Inherit the Wind*. New York: Dramatists Play Service, 2000 (reissue).

Nardo, Don. *The Origin of Species: Darwin's Theory of Evolution*. San Diego: Lucent Books, 2001.

Pietrusza, David. *The Roaring Twenties*. San Diego: Lucent Books, 1998.

Sherrow, Victoria. *Censorship in Schools*. Springfield, NJ: Enslow Publishers, 1996.

WEB SITES

Five Educational Philosophies: Progressivism. http://edweb.sdsu.edu/people/Lshaw/F95syll/philos/phprogr.html (accessed on August 2, 2002).

John Dewey (1859–1952). http://www.philosophypages.com/ph/dewe.htm (accessed on August 2, 2002).

1920s. http://www.richland2.org/svh/Media/socstud/1920s.htm (accessed on August 5, 2002).

Scopes Trial Home Page. http://www.law.umkc.edu/faculty/projects/ftrials/scopes/scopes.htm (accessed on August 2, 2002).

Government, Politics, and Law

1920: The 1920 census reports that 105,710,620 people live in the United States. For the first time, urban dwellers outnumber rural residents.

1920: January 16 Prohibition of the manufacture, sale, and transportation of alcoholic beverages goes into effect.

1920: May 8–14 The Socialist Party nominates Eugene V. Debs as its presidential candidate. Debs had been in prison since 1918 for violating the Espionage Act.

1921: June 20 Alice Robertson becomes the first woman to preside over the U.S. House of Representatives. She remains at the podium for thirty minutes. A middle school in Muskogee, Oklahoma, later is named in her honor.

1921: June 30 President Warren G. Harding appoints former president William Howard Taft as chief justice of the U.S. Supreme Court.

1921: November 2 Congress votes to designate November 11 a national holiday called Armistice Day.

1922: May 15 The U.S. Supreme Court declares the federal Child Labor Law unconstitutional.

1922: May 16 President Harding creates the Federal Narcotics Control Board.

1922: June 14 African Americans gather for a silent march in Washington, D.C. to show support for the Anti-Lynching Bill.

1922: October 3 Eighty-seven-year-old Rebecca Felton of Georgia becomes the first female U.S. senator. Her appointment, to take the place of her deceased son, lasts only one day.

1923: April 9 In *Adkins* v. *Children's Hospital,* the U.S. Supreme Court rules that the minimum wage law covering women and children is unconstitutional.

1923: September 15 Oklahoma governor J. C. Walton places his state under martial law to control racial violence caused by the white supremacist group, the Ku Klux Klan (KKK).

1924: March 10 J. Edgar Hoover is appointed acting director of the Federal Bureau of Investigation (FBI).

1924: April 15 The U.S. Senate unanimously votes to ban all Japanese immigrants, except ministers, educators, and their families.

1924: June 15 President Calvin Coolidge signs legislation granting U.S. citizenship to all Native Americans.

1924: September 1 The Dawes Plan goes into effect. It calls upon American bankers to loan money to Germany to assist the defeated nation in paying its war reparations.

1925: January 5 Nellie Taylor Ross of Wyoming becomes the first woman governor of a state when she completes her late husband's term.

1925: August 8 Forty thousand members of the KKK march on Washington, D.C., to gain support for their cause.

1926: February 26 President Coolidge signs the Revenue Act, reducing federal income taxes.

1926: March 3 The Senate ratifies a treaty with Mexico to prevent smuggling narcotics, liquor, and illegal aliens across the border.

1926: April 7 The U.S. Attorney General reports to the U.S. Senate Prohibition Committee that the national trade in illegal intoxicating liquors is estimated at $3.6 billion since the Volstead Act, which codified the Proibition amendment, was passed in 1919.

1927: The Kellogg-Briand Pact is drafted, renouncing war as an option for resolving international disputes. Eventually, sixty-two nations will sign the pact.

1927: April 6 President Coolidge vetoes a resolution from the legislature of the Philippines declaring its independence from the United States.

1927: November 21 The U.S. Supreme Court upholds the right of the state of Mississippi to place all nonwhite students in "colored" public schools.

1928: June 4 The U.S. Supreme Court upholds the right of federal agents to wiretap private telephones during investigations of individuals suspected of violating Prohibition laws.

1928: November 27 The Civil Service Commission announces that it will install fingerprinting systems in 250 cities "to keep the crooks out" of government employ.

1929: January 1 Franklin Delano Roosevelt is sworn in as governor of New York.

1929: October 29 The Dow Jones Industrial Average falls 30.57 points as the stock market crashes. $30 billion in market value evaporates on what comes to be known as "Black Tuesday."

※ *Overview*

At the beginning of the new decade, America was in a position to pursue world leadership through international trade and the spread of democracy. But instead of forming political and economic alliances with its allies from World War I (1914–18), America retreated into isolationism, avoiding entanglements in international affairs. The horror of World War I had clouded many Americans' vision of working with other countries, and political policy started to close off America from the rest of the world.

Seeking means to keep foreign elements from crossing American borders, the government restricted immigration. Whereas immigrants had been welcomed during the 1910s as a fresh stock of workers who could be "Americanized" to become good citizens, foreigners were now "dangers" to be kept away from the United States. Immigrants were viewed as competitors for jobs. They were shunned as political or religious outsiders, and even feared as radicals who threatened the American lifestyle.

On the domestic front, people were becoming more distrustful of others whose religions or cultures differed from their own. This growing provincialism (a limited or unsophisticated outlook) placed factions against one another. White Anglo-Saxon Protestants (WASPs) clashed with blacks, Catholics, and Jews. The white separatist supremacist group known as the Ku Klux Klan (KKK) was revived, and wreaked havoc among minorities in the South, particularly African Americans. As provincialism spread, the mainly Protestant Prohibitionists (those who supported outlawing the manufacture, distribution, and consumption of alcoholic beverages) from rural areas viewed big-city dwellers with fear and distrust. Many of these blind hatreds spilled over into the political arena.

The shift in Americans' attitudes caused a similar shift in political power. By the end of the 1910s, Democratic President Woodrow Wilson had lost party support in a Congress which had become strongly Republican. The situation made it impossible for Wilson's post-World War I policies to be enacted. As the 1920s unfolded, Washington D.C. became a Republican stronghold. Republican presidential candidate Warren G. Harding won a landslide victory in 1920. Upon Harding's sudden death in 1923, Vice President Calvin Coolidge assumed the presidency. His election to a full term as president in 1924 assured the continuance of Republican Party policy. When Coolidge stepped aside in 1928, he paved the way for fellow Republican Herbert Hoover to take over the presidency. Throughout the decade, the Republicans held majorities in both houses of Congress.

The Republicans established a probusiness approach that lasted throughout the decade. Government intervention in business matters was minimized. The federal government cut back on spending and allowed generous tax cuts. In general, the policies pleased the public. One exception was the agricultural community, whose members suffered substantially from lack of federal support.

With close ties between big business and government, scandals and corruption marred the 1920s. President Harding's attorney general Harry Daugherty left office over allegations of corruption, and then the director of the Veterans' Bureau stepped down over charges of fraud. The decade's most sensational scandal was the Teapot Dome affair, in which Albert Fall, Harding's secretary of the interior, took bribes in exchange for awards of oil leases. In 1923, he and Secretary of the Navy Edwin Denby resigned in disgrace over this matter.

The greatest example of the dramatic change in America during the 1920s is Prohibition. The enactment of the Eighteenth Amendment to the Constitution in 1919 forbade the sale or use of alcohol in America. During the 1920s, Prohibition split the country into opposing factions: those who favored a "dry" lifestyle or those who condemned it. Prohibition led to the underground sale of alcoholic beverages through organized crime syndicates. The illegal trade in "bootleg gin" made gangsters as famous as movie stars and turned mob bosses into millionaires.

Alphonse "Al" Capone (1899–1947) Alphonse "Al" Capone was the most notorious gangster of the Prohibition era. Born in Brooklyn, New York, Capone moved to Chicago in 1915. By murdering the competition, he rose through the gangland's organization to assume control. A racketeer and bootlegger (producer and distributor of illegal intoxicating liquors), Capone amassed a fortune estimated in 1929 at $50 million. His most infamous crime was the St. Valentine's Day Massacre of February 14, 1929, a bloody assassination of a rival gang at a Chicago garage. *Photo reproduced by permission of Archive Photos, Inc.*

Calvin Coolidge (1872–1933) Republican Calvin Coolidge rose to the presidency upon the death of Warren G. Harding in 1923. Upon taking office, Coolidge distanced himself from Harding and cleaned up the scandals which had involved members of the previous administration. Nicknamed "Silent Cal," Coolidge lacked vision and leadership skills. Still, he was elected to a full term in 1924. A supporter of big business and high tariffs, Coolidge kept taxes low and restricted immigration. Choosing to run a government of nonintervention, Coolidge implied the source of leadership should come from industry when he declared, "The business of America is business." *Photo reproduced courtesy of the Library of Congress.*

Clarence Darrow (1857–1938) Clarence Darrow was one of the most renowned and effective trial lawyers of the early twentieth century. He often chose to defend the underdog against powerful opponents. Early in the century, he took the side of union organizers against big business. During World War I, Darrow defended antiwar dissidents accused of violating sedition laws. His most publicized cases include the Leopold and Loeb murder trial, Scopes's teaching of evolution, and the African American Sweet family's defense for firing guns into a white mob that was storming their home. *Photo reproduced courtesy of the Library of Congress.*

Warren G. Harding (1865–1923) With his landslide election to the U.S. presidency in 1920, Ohio Republican Warren G. Harding ushered in a spirit of laissez-faire politics, a doctrine which downplayed government intervention in economic matters. His administration popularized the term "normalcy." Harding's policies promoted an expansion of American business, and among his advisers were top businessmen. Harding was a charismatic man whose sudden death on August 2, 1923 during a transcontinental lecture tour cast a pall over the nation. *Photo reproduced courtesy of the Library of Congress.*

Herbert Hoover (1874–1964) For most of the 1920s, Herbert Hoover served as secretary of commerce, first in the Harding and later in the Coolidge administration. He successfully promoted cooperation between government and big business, balancing a laissez-faire approach with humanitarian values. Hoover began his single term as president in 1929. When the stock market crashed ten months into his term, he unwisely chose a policy of self-help to resolve the problems of the economy. This choice led to much woe during the Great Depression of the 1930s. To his shame, the makeshift Depression-era cities of shacks in which the homeless lived were nicknamed "Hoovervilles." *Photo reproduced courtesy of the Library of Congress.*

Robert M. La Follette (1855–1925) Reform-minded politician Robert La Follette went from the Wisconsin governor's mansion to become U.S. senator from 1906 until his death in 1925. A member of the progressive wing of the Republican Party, La Follette opposed big business interests and other policies that improved the lot of the privileged classes. He opposed child labor, and he attempted to unite agricultural interests with organized labor. La Follette contested America's entry into World War I and the postwar plan for a League of Nations. He became a third-party candidate for president in 1924, representing the Progressive Party. Many of the reforms for which he fought were enacted as laws after his death. *Photo reproduced courtesy of the Corbis Corporation.*

Andrew W. Mellon (1855–1937) Pittsburgh-based financier and industrialist Andrew W. Mellon served as secretary of the treasury during three presidential administrations, from 1921 to 1931. In this role, he used his outstanding business acumen to reduce the national debt by approximately $9 billion. Advocating economy in federal spending, Mellon used his high-level commercial connections to keep communications flowing between big business and the government. A multimillionaire with a philanthropic bent, he founded the Mellon Institute of Industrial Research and donated his renowned art collection to form the foundation of the National Gallery of Art in Washington, D.C. *Photo reproduced by permission of Archive Photos, Inc.*

Alfred E. Smith (1873–1944) Alfred E. Smith was raised in poverty on New York City's Lower East Side and attained only an eighth-grade formal education. He joined New York City's Democratic Party, and eventually he was elected representative to the state assembly. He then served two terms as governor of New York starting in 1918. Throughout his career, Smith worked to improve lifestyles of working-class people by regulating labor conditions and workers' compensation, developing low-cost housing and a parks and recreation system, and assuring civil liberties. An Irish Catholic, Smith became a controversial, and ultimately unsuccessful, presidential candidate in 1928. *Photo reproduced by permission of Archive Photos, Inc.*

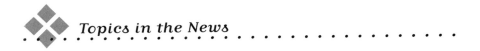

Topics in the News

❖ ISOLATIONISM AND INFIGHTING

During 1918 and 1919, Democratic president Woodrow Wilson (1856–1924) stressed the importance of international peace. He emphasized a no-guilt peace settlement, and he urged the development of a League of Nations to resolve disagreements without violence. These principles, outlined in Wilson's Fourteen Points, a list of postwar goals, failed to gain U.S. support. By war's end, Congress had a Republican majority which defeated the president's aims for international relations. Despite Wilson's involvement in the negotiations and his firm support of the Treaty of Versailles, which formally ended World War I, the United States never signed the treaty and did not become a member of the newly established League of Nations.

As the new decade began, the Republican Party moved into the executive branch of government with the nation's enthusiastic election of Republican Warren G. Harding (1865–1923) to the presidency in 1920. The changing character of government was a reflection of the public's move backwards into isolationism and provincialism (a limited or unsophisticated outlook). After several years of participating in international warfare, the public pulled back from the world, as an injured animal retreats into a corner to lick its wounds. Additionally, Americans retreated from one another, with a growing distrust for people different from themselves.

The country became divided along sharp political, religious, and ethnic lines. One of the greatest wedges driving Americans apart was the fear of communists, a hysteria which became known as the Red Scare. On January 2, 1920, U.S. Attorney General A. Mitchell Palmer (1872–1936) instructed federal agents to raid pool halls, restaurants, and private homes in thirty-three cities. More than four thousand people were arrested as alleged communists and radicals. Casting aside civil liberties, Palmer detained many suspects without proper warrants. The Palmer raids resulted in the imprisonment and deportation of many foreign-born residents and instilled in Americans a national hysteria. Many feared that a "red menace," or communist enemy, was living among them.

At the time, there were three separate communist parties within the United States. All were blamed for a downturn in the economy, when in fact the industrial and business problems at the start of the 1920s could be traced to the shift from a wartime to a peacetime economy. As organized labor pushed for wage increases and improved working conditions, it was the communists whom Americans blamed for labor disputes. Additionally, during 1919 bombs were sent to thirty-six U.S. government officials; these actions also were blamed on the communists and radical groups. By the end of 1920, however, the violence had subsided, and Americans began realizing that the "red scare" was exaggerated.

Nevertheless, the fear of "different" people continued to pervade public opinion throughout the decade. Immigrants were perceived by many Anglo-Saxon Protestant Americans in two ways: as competitors in the postwar slumping job market who would work for low wages, and as radical outsiders bent on destroying the American way of life. The image of the United States as a safe harbor for foreigners had been destroyed. In 1921, legislation began to limit the steady flow of foreigners into the United States. That year, an emergency immigration restriction act held the number of immigrants to 355,000 per year. Each foreign country was assigned a quota: 3 percent of the number of people from that country already in the United States according to the 1910 census.

As the economy recovered, American businesses needed immigrants as cheap labor. Still, the public's negative view towards foreigners did not change. Racial theorists began to spout ideas that white Anglo-Saxon Americans were superior to the mix of immigrants of various races and ethnicities whose characteristics and cultures were stirred into one great American "melting pot." Many influential Anglo-Saxon Americans listened to these theories and pressured Congress to pass further legislation to restrict immigration. In 1924, Congress passed the National Origins Act which further limited the number of Europeans entering the United States to 150,000 per year. The quota for each nation was lowered to 2 percent of foreign-born persons from that country who already lived in the United States at the time of the 1890 census. That change especially affected the number of southern and eastern Europeans who could enter, since many from countries in those regions had not arrived in the United States until after 1890. In an additional attempt to exclude those who were different, the federal government enacted a law during the 1920s to keep out all Asian immigrants.

The public's fear of foreigners provided fertile ground for the revival of the Ku Klux Klan (KKK), a white supremacist organization. Part of the motivation for the resurgence of the Klan lay with widespread beliefs of Anglo-Saxon racial superiority; part lay with the popularity of the epic film *The Birth of a Nation* (1915), which glorified the Klan's activities. The new KKK did not limit its violence and intimidations to African Americans in the South. Klan members also targeted Catholics, Jews, and immigrants. The U.S. House of Representatives investigated Klan activities, but very little came of the inquiry, due to the supremacist group's sweeping power. During the early 1920s Klan support of political candidates influenced many elections. Later in the decade, however, the authority of the Klan diminished because the majority of Americans did not share the KKK's hatreds. Furthermore, publicized murders by Klan members eventually were recognized as gruesome and repulsive crimes.

❖ PROHIBITION

The Volstead Act, passed in 1919, codified the newly ratified Eighteenth Amendment to the U.S. Constitution which banned the production, transportation, and sale of intoxicating liquor in the United States. Intoxicating liquor meant any drink containing at least 0.5 percent alcohol, thus placing beer among the forbidden beverages. Existing supplies of intoxicants could be used only for medicinal and religious purposes.

Prohibition split the nation into two groups: the mainly Anglo-Saxon Protestant middle class who were pleased to have a "dry" nation and the ethnic and immigrant working class who were anti-Prohibitionists. Many Americans who did not agree with the Volstead Act supported illegal

OPPOSITE PAGE
Ku Klux Klan members carrying torches and burning a large cross in a Mississippi field. The KKK was revived during the 1910s and 1920s.
Reproduced by permission of AP/Wide World Photos.

"speakeasies," which were concealed bars run by members of organized crime syndicates. Many of the gangsters who ran the speakeasies became rich from selling "bootleg gin." One of the most notorious of the "bootleggers" was Al Capone (1899–1947) who provided illegal liquor to the

Chicago area. Organized crime was rampant throughout the nation, and the government could not supply enough police to shut down the illegal liquor trade. Many gangsters and innocent bystanders were maimed or killed in street shootouts among rival gangs.

During the decade, Governor Alfred E. Smith (1873–1944) of New York was one of many outspoken opponents of Prohibition. Smith argued that Prohibition was sparking the spread of organized crime, was an unnatural lifestyle for many Americans, and was difficult to enforce. Anti-Prohibitionists attempted to convince the government that taxes on legally manufactured intoxicating liquors would boost the economy. Eventually, the Volstead Act was repealed by the enactment of the Twenty-First Amendment, and Prohibition ended in 1933.

❖ GOVERNMENT AND BUSINESS

As the decade began, the U.S. economy was in a short-lived recession. Inflation (the continuing rise in the general price of goods and services because of an overabundance of available money) was under control, but the unemployment rate stayed between 3 and 4 percent. From 1922 through 1927, the economy grew at a healthy rate of 7 percent per year. Industry and manufacturing increased as demand and consumption grew.

Republican presidents Warren G. Harding, Calvin Coolidge, and Herbert Hoover took the stance that government should not intervene in the business of big business. In fact, in 1925 Coolidge declared, "The business of America is business. The man who builds a factory builds a temple. The man who works there worships there." Material success became a measuring stick for a person's leadership ability. Being poor implied that a person had not taken advantage of opportunities. Therefore, business leaders were viewed as respected national leaders. It was this philosophy that drove Secretary of the Treasury Andrew W. Mellon (1855–1937) to keep out of the way of big business. Mellon discouraged government spending, and he cut taxes. He felt that removing the tax burden from the wealthy would spark industrialists to expand manufacturing, and eventually their gains would trickle down to provide more jobs to the labor class.

The U.S. Commerce Department, which Hoover headed before becoming president, emphasized a balance of unregulated business interests with humanitarian values. Hoover relied on corporate leadership to promote efficiency and self-regulation. Meanwhile, unions were losing members and power. In 1920 unions boasted 5.1 million members; by 1929 they had only 3.6 million. Without government regulation, businesses were not obligated to give benefits to their employees. Throughout the 1920s, owners offered laborers "welfare capitalism," a paternalistic system of services that pacified many employees. However, these benefits were only voluntary packages which often were reduced or rescinded by owners when employees tried to use them.

❖ GOVERNMENT AND AGRICULTURE

Farmers suffered during the 1920s. Production was high, but so were production costs. Many farmers incurred huge debts. Surpluses abounded, and the price of commodities (products of agriculture) remained low. Meanwhile, the costs of land, machinery, equipment, labor, and transportation all rose. These imbalances destroyed farmers' profits.

The supply of farm products outstripped the demand. That problem was not easily detectable at the time, however. The agricultural community instead pinned its failure to make profits on insufficient credit, high interest rates, inadequate tariffs (duties on imported or exported goods), and a decline in international trade. As the nation's population poured out of the countryside into the cities, rural farming areas lost the attention of government. Even so, some congressional leaders tried to deal with farm problems during the decade. During President Harding's administration, a "farm-bloc" was organized to exert pressure to legislate the farmers out of their predicament. This caucus (a group that unites to promote a cause) advocated extending generous credit to farmers, combined with high tariffs and cooperative marketing. While these proposals treated the symptoms, they did not solve the long-term problems of the farmers.

Then George N. Peek (1873–1943) of the Moline Plow Company suggested a plan to achieve economic equality for agriculture by adjusting farm prices to match the more prosperous farm period of 1909 to 1914. Congress adapted Peek's idea into a federal price support system for agricultural products. The McNary-Haugen Bill was argued for three years, and when it finally reached President Coolidge's desk in 1927, he vetoed it. When President Hoover came into office, however, he signed into law subsequent farm-related legislation. The Agricultural Marketing Act followed Hoover's guidelines for self-help, as opposed to federally legislated assistance for farmers. The bill did not bring effective results, however, and farmers faced many more years of unresolved problems.

❖ NATIONAL POLITICS: THE ELECTIONS OF THE 1920S

Throughout the decade, the Republican Party controlled the federal government. The three U.S. presidents to follow Democrat Woodrow Wilson (1856–1924) into office were all Republicans. Both houses of Congress had gained Republican majorities by the end of the 1910s. During the 1920s, some Congressional seats would return to Democrats, but Republicans maintained the majority vote.

During the final months of his second term, incumbent President Wilson was embittered by the lack of Congressional support for his post-World War I international peace plan. In his frustration, he delayed announcing his candidacy for a third term. His hesitation made other potential Democratic candidates reluctant to come forward, not wanting to challenge a seated president. Having suffered two strokes, Wilson needed to face the fact of his failing health. Still, he did not step down.

By the time the Democratic National Convention began in San Francisco on June 28, 1920, Wilson still had not decided whether to seek a third term. Among other Democrats who were running were Secretary of the Treasury and Wilson's son-in-law William McAdoo, Governor James M. Cox of Ohio, Attorney General A. Mitchell Palmer, Governor Alfred E. Smith of New York, and Senator Carter Glass of Virginia. After several ballots, Cox finally gained the nomination. The Assistant Secretary of the Navy, Franklin Delano Roosevelt (1882–1945), was the vice-presidential nominee.

The Republicans chose Warren G. Harding (1865–1923) and Calvin Coolidge (1872–1933) as their presidential and vice-presidential nominees. Rather than wage a campaign on the issues, Harding chose to run on the basis of his image. Campaigning from his front porch in Marion, Ohio, he presented himself as a down-home man wanting peace and "normalcy" for the United States. A former newspaper publisher, Harding enlisted the support of 90 percent of newspaper editors across the country. Coolidge was a quiet man who followed Harding's lead, campaigning for patriotism and common sense in government. The Republican ticket won a landslide victory, capturing 404 electoral votes to just 127 for the Democrats.

Harding's ineffectiveness during his first two years in office sparked an outpouring of Democratic voters during the interim elections of 1922. Democrats retained all their congressional seats and gained an additional seventy that had been held by Republicans. Still, the Republicans made up the majority.

Harding's sudden death in August 1923 had placed Calvin Coolidge in the Oval Office. He ran for reelection in 1924 as the Republican incumbent. Charles G. Dawes (1865–1951), a conservative who opposed organized labor, ran as Coolidge's vice president.

Uplifted by the results of the congressional elections of 1922, Democrats hoped for a presidential victory in 1924. Unfortunately, their most promising candidate, William McAdoo (1863–1941), was involved in the

Women Succeed in Joining the Electorate

The Nineteenth Amendment to the Constitution was passed in June 1919 and ratified by the states by August 1920. It reads, "The right of citizens of the United States to vote shall not be denied or abridged by the United States or any State on account of sex."

At first, many women were hesitant to exercise their right to vote. Of those who did, the majority timidly echoed the political leanings of their husbands or other family males. To bring females to the polls, the League of Women Voters, founded in 1920, disseminated educational pamphlets about upcoming elections and encouraged women to actively participate in politics. After their initial reluctance, women enthusiastically began to participate in the electoral process.

Teapot Dome scandal and connected to the Ku Klux Klan, a group which attracted many rural dwellers but was shunned by urbanites. McAdoo's opponent for the Democratic nomination was Alfred E. Smith (1873–1944). The two fought for the nomination but neither could get the necessary two-thirds majority. Finally, a compromise candidate was chosen on the 103rd ballot: John W. Davis (1873–1955), a lawyer and former U.S. ambassador to Great Britain. Davis ran on "The American Creed" platform, which minimized government intervention in business and was similar to Coolidge's position. Davis' vice-presidential running mate was Governor Charles W. Bryan (1867–1945) of Nebraska.

A third party candidate, Senator Robert La Follette (1855–1925), left the Republican Party to run on behalf of the Progressive Party. That party's campaign platform opposed monopolies and called for public ownership of water power, the nationalization of railroads, increased taxes of the wealthy, and an end to child labor. La Follette distanced himself from the Communist Party and denounced the Klan. Davis, too, denounced the Klan. Only Coolidge refused to take a stance on the KKK. Coolidge returned to office with 382 electoral votes; Davis won 136 electoral votes from the solid Democratic South. La Follette carried only Wisconsin but received 17 percent of the popular vote nationwide.

Congressional elections brought the Democrats seven new seats. Coolidge experienced some embarrassment when his fellow Republican,

Senator William Butler (1861–1937) of Coolidge's home state of Massachusetts, and the only candidate with whom he personally campaigned, was defeated. Despite the Democratic gains, however, Republicans still held the majority of votes in Congress.

The economy was booming, yet Calvin Coolidge refused to run for reelection in 1928. Endorsing the current president's policies, Herbert Hoover (1874–1964) of California stepped forward to seek the presidency. He was nominated on the first ballot at the Republican Party's national convention. Charles Curtis (1860–1936) of Kansas was his vice-presidential running mate.

The divided Democratic Party realized it would be necessary to win the electoral votes of New York, so the Democrats chose New York's Governor Alfred E. Smith as their candidate. Because Smith was an Irish Catholic running for a job that previously had been won only by Protestants, he was controversial. Additionally, Smith was a liberal who opposed Prohibition. Many in the party hoped that conservative Democrat McAdoo would come forward to oppose Smith, but he did not do so. Smith ran with vice-presidential nominee Joseph T. Robinson (1872–1937) of Arkansas.

Smith urged voters to reopen immigration and repeal Prohibition. Although he stressed the separation of church and state, many Americans saw his Catholicism as troublesome. Some viewed him as a radical with leanings toward New York's corrupt Tammany Hall political machine, a loyalty he did not deny. Americans even criticized his wife for lacking social graces and talking too much!

In the end, Republican Hoover won the election with an impressive 444 electoral votes. Smith garnered the support of only eight states with a total of eighty-seven electoral votes. Despite the disappointing outcome, Smith actually won 41 percent of the popular vote and helped advance Democratic Party policies in a number of cities.

❖ THE TEAPOT DOME SCANDAL

Although several scandals burdened the presidency of Warren Harding, the most highly publicized was the Teapot Dome controversy. The situation involved three U.S. Naval oil reserve stations that President Wilson had set up for government use only. Two of them were in California, and one was in Teapot Dome, Wyoming. In 1921, Secretary of the Interior and anticonservationist Albert B. Fall (1861–1944), arranged with Secretary of the Navy Edwin Denby (1870–1929) to have the rights to the naval oil reserves transferred to the Department of the Interior. Fall then quietly granted drilling rights at one California station to Edward L. Doheny (1856–1935), owner of

By 1920, the U.S. census showed that for the first time, more Americans were living in cities than in rural areas. Because the population had shifted dramatically to urban centers, a need arose for reapportionment (a reconfiguration of congressional districts). Congress failed to pass a vote to adjust seats, particularly due to the strenuous opposition of rural-based congressmen who feared they would lose their positions. Not until 1929 would Congress pass a bill authorizing the president to reapportion districts if Congress failed to do so.

the Pan-American Petroleum and Transport Company. Fall licensed the rights to drill at Elk Hills, California and at Teapot Dome to Harry Sinclair (1876–1956), owner of the Mammoth Oil Company.

After several conservationists heard about Fall's covert maneuvers, they asked assistance from Senator La Follette to launch a congressional investigation. Private hearings were followed by public hearings. Eventually, Fall resigned his position and then Harding died, diminishing the urgency of the investigation. However, the scandal did not remain dormant for long. When Fall began spending large sums of money, his friend Doheny admitted he was the source of "loans" to the former interior secretary. National attention was placed on the scandal, and several top Republicans resigned from their respective offices.

State trials proved that Fall had accepted bribes. He became the first cabinet member to serve a prison sentence for wrongdoing, but Sinclair and Doheny were acquitted. In 1924, Coolidge established the Federal Oil Conservation Board (FOCB) to promote the preservation of government oil supplies, and Hoover later announced the "complete conservation of government oil in this administration."

❖ THE HALL-MILLS MURDER CASE

The decade was sprinkled with well-publicized crimes. Among the most notorious was the Hall-Mills murder case. On September 16, 1922, the mutilated bodies of a man and woman were spotted underneath a crabapple tree near New Brunswick, New Jersey. The man was Reverend

Edward Wheeler Hall (1881–1922), a married man and rector of a fashionable Episcopalian church in New Brunswick. The woman was Eleanor Mills (c. 1888–1922), a married woman and member of the church choir. Their love letters were scattered around the murder site. Hall's widow and her brothers were heirs to the multimillion dollar Johnson and Johnson pharmaceutical company fortune. At first, the investigation was bungled and no charges were brought. Then in 1926, the case was reopened during a circulation war between two New York City tabloid newspapers. A pig farmer known as "The Pig Woman" claimed to have seen a couple struggling with a heavyset woman, like Mrs. Hall, and three men, possibly Mrs. Hall's two brothers and a cousin, on the night of the murder. In the end, all the defendants were acquitted. They sued one of the tabloids for $3 million in damages and were awarded an out-of-court settlement.

❖ *BUCK* V. *BELL:* EUGENICS AND PUBLIC POLICY

During the decade, a number of social commentators decried babies being born to people of inferior genes. Their reasoning was based on the science of eugenics (the improvement of the hereditary quality of the human race through selective breeding practices). People who believe in this science discount any role environment might play in determining a person's characteristics and behavior.

"Feeble-minded" women of child-bearing age often were placed in mental institutions or involuntarily sterilized. In 1924, Carrie Buck (1906–1983), a poverty-stricken white teenager subsequently deemed mentally retarded, was described as "morally delinquent" after becoming pregnant as a result of being raped. In January 1925 she bore a daughter who was adopted and subsequently developed into a healthy and mentally competent woman. After the birth Carrie was scheduled for sterilization surgery. On the basis of derogatory remarks made about Buck's parents, a court case followed. Buck's lawyer claimed her impending sterilization was the result of social prejudice. The case eventually went before the U.S. Supreme Court, which ruled on May 2, 1927, that Buck's forced sterilization was legal and necessary for the general public good. After the decision, twenty states instituted eugenics laws. Four decades later, the decision was reversed.

*OPPOSITE PAGE
Nathan Leopold and
Richard Loeb being
escorted from the county
jail after being found
guilty by reason of
insanity for kidnapping
and murdering fourteen-
year-old Robert Franks.
Reproduced by permission of
AP/Wide World Photos.*

❖ THE LEOPOLD AND LOEB CASE

On May 21, 1924, Nathan Leopold (1904–1971) and Richard Loeb (1905–1936), two academically brilliant teenagers from wealthy Jewish families in Chicago, lured fourteen-year-old Robert Franks (1910–1924), into their automobile. After bludgeoning him to death, they half-buried his body in a railway culvert (a transverse drain) at a public park. They then called Frank's parents to ask for $10,000 in ransom for the return of their son. The murderers imagined they had carried out the "perfect crime."

The Schwimmer Case:
No Citizenship for Conscientious Objectors

In August 1921 Professor Rosika Schwimmer (1877–1948), a Hungarian Jew, entered the United States to take a teaching position at the University of Chicago. After five years as a resident alien, she applied for U.S. citizenship. On the application form, Schwimmer, a noted pacifist, answered no to a question about being willing to bear arms during any future national emergency. Because of this response, she was denied citizenship by the U.S. Department of State. Schwimmer sued the federal government, and on April 12, 1929, the U.S. Supreme Court ruled against her. Justice Pierce Butler (1866–1939) spoke for the majority by declaring, "The influence of conscience objectors against the use of military force in defense...of our Government is apt to be more detrimental than the mere refusal to bear arms."

Unfortunately for them, Loeb had left his prescription sunglasses near the body. Renowned attorney Clarence Darrow (1857–1938) defended the teens, who had confessed but appeared arrogant during the trial. Believing that neither Leopold nor Loeb had any sense of right or wrong, Darrow set out to prove that his clients were indeed guilty, but insane. He did so in order to save the two men from the death penalty. Darrow's approach worked, and Leopold and Loeb were given life sentences. In 1936, Loeb was killed during a prison brawl. In 1958, Leopold was paroled. He married in 1961 and died ten years later.

❖ RACE RELATIONS

In February 1925, Ossian Sweet (1895–1960), an African American physician, moved with his family to a white neighborhood in Detroit, Michigan. Neighbors protested the presence of a black family by vandalizing the Sweet home. Sweet surrounded his family with black bodyguards and announced that he owned an arsenal of weapons. On September 9, a riot ensued with whites storming the front porch of the Sweet residence and smashing several windows. The Sweets fired guns into the mob; one rioter was killed. Sweet claimed that he had given warning. The Sweets and their bodyguards were charged with murder and armed assault. The National Association for the Advancement of Colored People (NAACP) raised $75,000 for the defense expenses. Arthur Garfield Hays (1881–1954) and

Clarence Darrow were the defense lawyers, and the jury was racially mixed. By pointing out conflicts in onlookers' accounts, Darrow discredited several witnesses. Meanwhile, the prosecution was unable to prove the murder was premeditated. No convictions were made. The Sweet trial was an exception to the many "Jim Crow" convictions of the period.

In 1925, a Chinese American student was denied entrance to a white high school in Mississippi on the basis of her race. She was instructed to apply to the inferior quality "colored" high school in the next county. Her family's lawyer argued that the girl did not belong in the "colored" school, stating that "Colored describes only one race, and that is the Negro." In late 1927, the U.S. Supreme Court ruled unanimously that "colored" referred to "all members of the brown, yellow, red, and black races."

❖ THE SACCO AND VANZETTI CASE

On April 15, 1920, the paymaster of a factory in Massachusetts was robbed of more than $15,000 and killed, along with another victim. The armed robbers later were described by witnesses as "two short, dark, foreign types." The next month, state police picked up two Italian immigrants in a raid: Nicola Sacco (1891–1927) and Bartolomeo Vanzetti (1888–1927). Both were anarchists and union organizers. Police found a gun in Sacco's possession, and ballistic experts later claimed that bullets fired from the gun matched those found in the victims. At the subsequent trial, several witnesses identified the immigrants as the criminals, but most of the evidence was circumstantial. Sacco and Vanzetti were found guilty and sentenced to death by electrocution.

Their lawyer managed to delay their death for several years, during which time many American liberals and intellectuals protested the arrest and conviction of the anarchists as a "political prosecution" indicative of anti-immigrant, anti-establishment feelings. Eventually the U.S. Supreme Court ruled against a stay of execution, and in 1927 Sacco and Vanzetti were electrocuted. In 1977, Massachusetts Governor Michael Dukakis (1933–) issued a proclamation essentially absolving Sacco and Vanzetti of the crime.

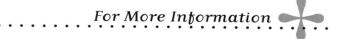

For More Information

BOOKS

Allen, Frederick Lewis. *Only Yesterday: An Informal History of the 1920s.* New York: Perennial Classics, 2000 (reprint edition).

Altman Linda Jacobs. *The Decade That Roared: America During Prohibition.* New York: Twenty-First Century Books, 1997.

Andryszewski, Tricia. *Immigration: Newcomers and Their Impact on the United States.* Brookfield, CT: Millbrook Press, 1995.

Clinton, Susan. *Herbert Hoover.* Chicago: Children's Press, 1988.

Feinstein, Stephen. *The 1920s: From Prohibition to Charles Lindbergh.* Berkeley Heights, NJ: Enslow Publishers, 2001.

Feuerlicht, Roberta Strauss. *America's Reign of Terror: World War I, the Red Scare, and the Palmer Raids.* New York: Random House, 1971.

Hesse, Karen. *Witness.* New York: Scholastic Trade, 2001.

Hintz, Martin. *Farewell, John Barleycorn: Prohibition in the United States.* Minneapolis: Lerner Publications, 1996.

Holford, David M. *Herbert Hoover.* Berkeley Heights, NJ: Enslow Publishers, 1999.

Lucas, Eileen. *The Eighteenth and Twenty-First Amendments: Alcohol-Prohibition and Repeal.* Springfield, NJ: Enslow Publishers, 1998.

Lutz, Norma Jean. *Battling the Klan.* Ulrichsville, OH: Barbour & Company, 1998.

Monroe, Judy. *The Sacco and Vanzetti Controversial Murder Trial: A Headline Court Case.* Berkeley Heights, NJ: Enslow Publishers, 2000.

Pietrusza, David. *The Roaring Twenties.* San Diego: Lucent Books, 1998.

Thorndike, Jonathan L. *The Teapot Dome Scandal Trial: A Headline Court Case.* Berkeley Heights, NJ: Enslow Publishers, 2001.

Trespacz, Karen L. *The Trial of Gangster Al Capone: A Headline Court Case.* Berkeley Heights, NJ: Enslow Publishers, 2001.

White, G. Edward. *Oliver Wendell Holmes: Sage of the Supreme Court.* New York: Oxford University Press Children's Books, 2000.

WEB SITES

The Growth of the Federal Government in the 1920s. http://www.cato.org/pubs/journal/cj16n2-2.html (accessed on August 5, 2002).

1920s. http://www.richland2.org/svh/Media/socstud/1920s.htm (accessed on August 5, 2002).

1920s. http://www.usgennet.org/usa/il/state/alhn1920.html (accessed on August 5, 2002).

The 1920s: News and Politics. http://www.louisville.edu/~kprayb01/1920s-News-1.html (accessed on August 2, 2002).

chapter five

Lifestyles and Social Trends

1920: A new three-button sports jacket made of cartridge cloth, fabric used to hold powder charges during World War I, becomes a predecessor of the men's lightweight summer suit.

1920: January 16 The Volstead National Prohibition Act goes into effect, providing enforcement for the Eighteenth Amendment that prohibits the manufacture, sale, and transportation of intoxicating liquor.

1921: High-button shoes for men are replaced by oxfords, low-cut shoes with laces.

1921: March 4 Warren G. Harding becomes the first U.S. president to arrive at his inaugural ceremony in an automobile.

1921: May Construction begins on the Wrigley Building in Chicago. It will have a 32-story tower and 442,000 square feet of office space.

1921: September 8 The first Miss America pageant is held in Washington, D.C.

1922: Architectural delineator (artistic renderer) Hugh Ferriss draws and publishes his influential artwork of the four stages of skyscraper construction.

1922: The "slouch suit," with jacket bloused over a hip-level belt, becomes popular among women.

1922: May 5 Gabrielle "Coco" Chanel introduces Chanel No. 5, which will become the world's most famous perfume.

1922: May 30 The Lincoln Memorial, sculpted by Chester French, is dedicated in Washington, D.C.

1922: September 22 Congress passes the Cable Act, granting independent citizenship to married women.

1923: The upscale Bergdorf Goodman fashion store for women opens a ready-to-wear department at its original Fifth Avenue location in New York City.

1923: October 29 The African American musical revue *Runnin' Wild* opens in New York City, featuring an exuberant, jazzy dance called the Charleston.

1924: Fashionable men begin wearing blue blazers with round-toed oxfords.

1924: Heavy make-up and plucked, redrawn eyebrows become popular with women.

1924: Architect Louis Sullivan publishes his influential book *The Autobiography of an Idea.*

1924: September Gimbel Brothers opens an upscale clothing store, Saks & Company, later to be called Saks Fifth Avenue.

1925: Skirt hemlines rise to knee length.

1925: The Model T Ford reaches its lowest price of $260. It had sold for $950 in 1909.

1925: The Jewish Institute of Religion graduates its first class.

1925: **May 13** The Florida legislature passes a law requiring daily Bible reading in public schools.

1926: Two thousand people die from drinking poisoned liquor during the year, as the illegal liquor trade reportedly brings in $3.5 billion.

1926: French tennis player Jean René Lacoste, nicknamed "The Crocodile," introduces the short-sleeved knit Lacoste tennis, or polo, shirt with a crocodile emblem on the chest.

1927: Grauman's Chinese Theater, a legendary American movie palace, opens in Hollywood. The architectural theme is Oriental.

1927: A dance called the lindy hop is named for aviation hero Charles Lindbergh.

1927: **May 10** The Evangelical Church rules that only celibate women may be ordained as ministers.

1928: Architect R. Buckminster Fuller introduces his prefabricated Dymaxion House, a six-sided module suspended from a central utility mast with outer walls of glass.

1928: **January 1** The Milam Building opens in San Antonio, Texas. It is the first air-conditioned office building in the United States.

1928: **December 1** The Model J Duesenberg, one of America's most spectacular automobiles, is first presented at the New York Automobile Salon.

1929: During the year, American women purchase an average of one pound of face powder and eight rouge compacts apiece.

1929: **Fall** Designer Jean Patou drops skirt lengths to mid-calf, ushering in a new style for women's fashion in the 1930s.

1929: **October 16** The Federal Council of Churches of Christ pledges its support for the textile worker strikes in Elizabethton, Tennessee, and Gastonia, North Carolina.

1929: **October 29** Black Tuesday: The stock market crashes. Within weeks, unemployment rises from 700 thousand to 3.1 million.

※ *Overview* . . . .

The post-World War I (1914–18) era, which stretched through the 1920s, was a time of prosperity and new opportunities. The economy was flourishing, and the middle class was enjoying a higher standard of living. More young people were seeking higher education, and college and university campuses became prime spots for new fashion trends to emerge. Women were granted the right to vote and had many more possibilities for jobs and careers. These improvements gave many females, especially younger ones, a new sense of empowerment. The Volstead Act of 1920 kept intoxicating liquor from the public; however, homemade stills (machines to manufacture alcoholic beverages) and illegal saloons called "speakeasies" gave people an opportunity to indulge in an evening's escapade of illegal drinking and maybe a chance to perform one of the jazzy new dances such as the Charleston or the black bottom!

In this energetic environment, more Americans became fashion-conscious. The emphasis on style was not limited to the upper classes, nor was it restricted to certain types of clothing. Fashion trends touched every facet of American life, including clothing, jewelry, perfumes, cosmetics, appliances, urban design, and automobiles. According to a marketing study from Columbia University in 1928, "Fashion is one of the greatest forces in everyday life."

By the start of the decade, spreading the word about the latest fashion vogues was a straightforward matter. Advertisers could buy space in national magazines to highlight the latest clothing and accessories or spotlight the most attractive new home furnishings to potential customers. Movies showed Hollywood stars wearing the latest designer evening gowns from Paris or the current casual attire. Also on the silver screen, audiences could view the latest in home decoration and modern appliances. Later in the decade, radio became an influential forum for advertising new styles and products.

As viewpoints became more worldly and lifestyles more adventuresome, clothing became more daring. Women's hemlines rose from ankle-length to knee-length. Inspired by sensuous movie sirens such as Theda

Bara and Pola Negri, women took on new looks with the aid of powder, rouge, and eyebrow pencil. Paris, France remained the fashion capital of the western world, and innovative French, designers catered to affluent Americans. For the fashion-conscious with less buying power, copies of Paris originals could be bought for a fraction of the original price or sewn from McCall's patterns. Men's clothing became less dour, and young college men began wearing baggy pleated flannel slacks and long raccoon coats. Also, men bought more fashions designed specifically for sports and leisure activities.

Urban skyscrapers with sleek lines began to replace the neo-gothic high-rises of the previous decade. High-rise luxury apartment buildings began to take the place of residential brownstones and townhouses in many big cities, in order to meet more modern lifestyles. More than ever, Americans became interested in interior decoration. Home furnishings often reflected historic period, and households were decorated in copies of antiques. The kitchen often was the only room to have a modern look. There, newly devised cooking and cleaning appliances not only proved functional but also looked attractive.

As all aspects of life were changing, Americans were becoming less connected to organized religion. Instead of attending church services, many Americans spent weekends riding in automobiles and watching movies. Hobbies became more frivolous as the nation became preoccupied with fads ranging from crossword puzzles to dance marathons. A youth culture arose, and teenagers indulged in pastimes such as petting parties, shocking their more conservative elders.

To bring the public back to religion, leaders of organized faiths and zealous believers began interacting with popular culture. An attempt even was made to bring Jesus Christ into modern times in order to make him more relevant. In the best-selling book *The Man Nobody Knows*, by Bruce Barton, Christ was refashioned into a modern businessman and masculine outdoorsman who likes women!

The 1920s was a time of prosperity, leading to new energy, excitement, and flamboyance. Sadly, the exuberance ended when the stock market crashed in 1929, and the public turned away from games, frolic, and fashion to face the unemployment and discouragement of the Great Depression.

Bruce Barton (1886–1967) A minister's son, Bruce Barton applied the concepts of Christianity to his writings by presenting Jesus as a modern man. In his best-selling book *The Man Nobody Knows* (1925), Barton depicted Jesus as a strong outdoorsman and "the founder of modern business." With his unorthodox take on the gospel, Barton's intention was to bring readers back to the church. His works did rekindle many Americans' faith. He coined the phrase that became the Salvation Army's slogan: "A man may be down, but he's never out."

Hattie Carnegie (1886–1956) Businesswoman Hattie Carnegie coordinated with top Paris designers and her own American staff to bring haute couture (high fashion) to American women. Her custom fashions appealed to rich and famous women and sparked a multimillion dollar fashion empire. She was the first entrepreneur to sell ready-to-wear clothing and a custom line under a single label. Carnegie also was among the first to complement a clothing line with a separate line of accessories, jewelry, cosmetics, and perfume. *Photo reproduced courtesy of the Library of Congress.*

Gabrielle "Coco" Chanel (1883–1971) French fashion designer Gabrielle "Coco" Chanel ran a fashion empire. Since the 1920s, her visions of simplicity and functionality have influenced women's clothing styles throughout Europe and the United States. Staples of Chanel's fashion house include the simple black chemise dress and the Chanel suit with its short, open, collarless jacket. She began marketing her world-renowned Chanel No. 5 perfume in 1922. Chanel was born into poverty, the daughter of a poorhouse worker, lacking any social contacts. As a young adult, she learned how to network with the wealthy. *Photo reproduced by permission of Archive Photos, Inc.*

Albert Kahn (1869–1942) Called the father of the modern American factory, Albert Kahn designed notable industrial plants that were both practical and visually pleasing. At a time when respected architects were designing museums and monuments, Kahn was among the first to turn his attention to the industrial workplace. Among his most notable projects was the Ford Motor Company plant (1909–14) in Highland Park, Michigan, which combined under one roof all the assembly line processes that went into the construction of the Model T Ford. Between 1929 and 1932, Kahn directed the construction of 521 factories. *Photo reproduced courtesy of the Library of Congress.*

Aimee Semple McPherson (1890–1944) Sister Aimee, as she was called, was one of the few women in the United States to form her own religous denomination (an organization uniting several congregations). With a strong commitment to saving souls, she traveled the country preaching and eventually found a permanent site for her Full Square Gospel Church in Los Angeles in 1918. Her flamboyant speaking style and her private life which was filled with dubious publicity-seeking events attracted large crowds to her revival meetings. McPherson also became a radio celebrity, and in 1924 she opened station KFSG (Kall Full Square Gospel), the first full-time religious radio station. *Photo reproduced by permission of Archive Photos, Inc.*

Addison Mizner (1872–1933) Addison Mizner's most notable contributions are his architectural designs for the ornate mansions of Palm Beach, Florida. Mizner invested in the Florida real estate boom of the 1920s by designing the city of Boca Raton. When that boom turned to bust in 1926, Mizner abandoned Boca Raton for other projects, including The Cloisters at Sea Island, Georgia. His designs often have been criticized as garish and gaudy; however, Mizner's supporters included other top architects and designers of the decade. *Photo reproduced by permission of the Corbis Corporation.*

Emily Post (1872–1960) America's most famous authority on etiquette, Emily Post was brought up in a genteel Baltimore household where she was tutored by a governess. After graduating from Miss Graham's finishing school, she made her society debut and then married a wealthy businessman. In 1922, she authored her first book on the subject of etiquette. In it and subsequent writings, Post codified American manners and modified traditional etiquette to suit the exuberance of contemporary life. Her appeal was widespread and drew many middle-class readers. For many years, Post wrote a syndicated magazine column on etiquette, and in 1946 opened the Emily Post Institute in her pursuit to establish standards of politeness and decorum. *Photo reproduced by courtesy of the Library of Congress.*

William "Billy" Sunday (1862–1935) William "Billy" Sunday was the most famous revivalist preacher in the United States during the 1910s and early 1920s. He fused the concepts of Christianity and American patriotism, and he called for an end to drinking liquor. During the late 1920s, Sunday held flashy, earthy revival meetings along the "sawdust trail" of the South and Midwest, rather than in the more sophisticated Northern cities where he was viewed as vulgar and crude. Sunday became a millionaire preaching against the sin of "demon rum," but his wealth brought questions of unethical financial gain from "love offerings" he kept that should have gone to local organizing groups. *Photo reproduced by permission of the Corbis Corporation.*

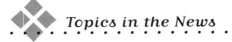

Topics in the News

❖ AN UPHEAVAL IN WOMEN'S FASHIONS

With the start of the decade came a sense of new freedom for women. The feeling of emancipation was due in part to the ratification of the Nineteenth Amendment in 1920, giving women the right to vote. Young females, in particular, sought more adventurous lifestyles. Whether they were homemakers or coeds, factory or office workers, teachers or nurses, young women were indulging in a variety of new activities shunned by the more old-fashioned older generation. They drove cars, played sports, and performed lively modern dances such as the Charleston and the black bottom. To suit the liberated attitudes of the day, modern females adopted a radical new look.

Women had their long hair cut or boyishly "bobbed" for freedom of movement and easy maintenance. They spurned the restrictions of corsets in favor of loose-bodiced tops that allowed maximum upper body movement and easier breathing. Early in the decade, hems boldly rose from ankle-length, or just above the ankle, to just below the knee, or mid-calf. With the new short skirts, hems no longer dragged in the dirt, and women could take longer strides. When dancing, a woman could kick and swing her legs without getting her skirt entangled in her shoes! Of course, lower leg exposure caused quite a panic among the more conservative members of American society.

From conservative magazines and religious pulpits came pronouncements that short skirts and bobbed hair were indicative of an immoral lifestyle. This unconventional "flapper" look was equated to such behavior as necking, dancing to jazz music, smoking, and drinking illegal liquor known as "bathtub gin." Novelist Fannie Hurst (1889–1968) defended the fashion trends as reflections of "the new psychological, sociological, economic and political status" of the young woman of the 1920s. Despite the controversy, the new look prevailed throughout the decade, although modifications arose through the years. For instance, early in the decade shorter haircuts were "marcelled" or waved. Later, a sleek helmet look became popular, and straight, flattened hairdos were worn with close-fitted bell-shaped "cloche" hats. Hemlines, too, had changed by mid-decade when more radical, knee-length skirts came into vogue.

Many fashions originated in Paris, where haute couture (high fashion) was adapted to meet American styles. Custom dress designers such as Gabrielle "Coco" Chanel, Madeline Vionnet, Paul Poiret, and Jean Patou sold their latest designs to department stores such as Bergdorf-Goodman, Lord & Taylor, and John Wanamaker. "Paris originals" would be purchased only by wealthy clients, since one evening gown might cost as much as $10,000. For

OPPOSITE PAGE
A magazine cover depicts young female flapper and an elderly man dancing the Charleston, a dance developed in the 1920s.
Reproduced by permission of the
Corbis Corporation.

the middle class, copies of designer gowns could be purchased at less elite stores such as B. Altman for approximately $100 to $250 per gown. For fashion-conscious women with less money to spend, McCall's sewing patterns, plus the purchase of fabric by the yard, presented an opportunity to make one's own Paris-inspired gown. Hemlines for formal evening wear were usually floor-length or a shorter mid-calf length with a petal-shaped hem.

For daywear, Chanel created her legendary tailored suit. The lines were simple and understated, with a soft pleated or straight skirt and a short, open, collarless jacket. She chose tweeds and jerseys as fabrics. Chanel also introduced the "little black dress" which began as a slightly blousy, plain number. Through the decades, the simple black dress has remained a fashion staple for informal but dressy occasions.

Women began having fun with accessories and started taking on new whimsical looks using cosmetics. They chose to wear T-strap pointed-toe shoes with one- to two-inch chunky heels. They often carried adorned metal cigarette cases and wore various styles of trendy jewelry. For instance, when the tomb of ancient Egyptian pharaoh Tutankhamen (c. 1370–1352 B.C.E.) was unearthed in 1922, American women accessorized their outfits with an Egyptian motif. When French avant-garde artwork became a topic of conversation, jewelry began mirroring abstract art movements such as cubism, art deco, and surrealism. Women altered their facial features with cosmetics to imitate movie stars. Some completely plucked their eyebrows and redrew them in dark eyebrow pencil. They even wore thick black eyeliner to take on a sensuous look popularized by movie stars Theda Bara (1890–1955) and Pola Negri (1894–1987). Later in the decade, young moderns traced the line of their lipstick to make "cupid-bow" lips like movie star Clara Bow (1905–1965).

During the previous decade, lingerie had progressed from whale-boned corsets and bustles that remolded a woman's body to underwear that reflected the natural form. During the 1920s, this trend continued as rubber girdles and brassieres came into fashion. Eventually, brassieres were made of more comfortable, breathable fabrics such as cotton, silk, and rayon (known as "artificial silk"). At that time, brassieres were meant to flatten a woman's breasts so that she could attain a boyish look. In 1923, Ida Cohen Rosenthal (1886–1973) introduced the more comfortable uplift brassiere through her company Maiden Form, which later became known as Maidenform. In addition, nude-colored rayon or silk stockings were worn above the knee and fastened with garters to a garter belt or girdle.

Adventurous and sports-minded women wore special outfits for each activity. For tennis, all-white short-skirted costumes were worn. For driving, some women adopted the look of World War I (1914–18) flying aces, donning leather jackets and large goggles. Swimsuits were clinging knit outfits that looked like modern one-piece bathing suits but extended further down the leg. The swimming costumes often were belted and sometimes the tops were striped at the breast or adorned with cubist art decorations such as floating circles, triangles, and squares.

❖ MEN'S FASHION BECOMES MORE CASUAL

During the 1920s, more than ever before, young men were attending colleges and universities. It was on campuses that men's fashion trends emerged. Because the new vogues were covered widely by magazines and newspapers, they spread throughout American society. Fashions were youthful and sporty, inspired by heroes of sports and aviation. Gentleman golfer Bobby Jones, tennis champion Bill Tilden, Olympic swimmer Johnny Weissmuller, and collegiate football star Red Grange set the standards for sports clothing. Through their influences, knickers and knee-high socks, two-colored saddle shoes, swimming trunks, full-length raccoon fur coats, and other sporty attire replaced the more conventional tweed sportswear of the previous decade. Later in the decade, dashing airplane pilot Charles Lindbergh (1902–1974) inspired men to attire themselves in leather jackets and silk scarves for driving.

Perhaps the most influential fashion trend setter of the decade was the heir to the British throne, Edward, Prince of Wales (1894–1972). When he made a tour of the United States in the autumn of 1924, his sharp fashion sense became apparent as he made public appearances in 1,819 different uniforms and suits and 3,601 distinct hats! For the next two decades,

Edward's choice of lapel-lines, cuffed or uncuffed slacks, and the number of buttons down the front of his suits would serve as guides for fashion-conscious American men.

Wide-shouldered suit coats of the previous decade were replaced by slim-fitting suits with no shoulder padding. Jackets were vented at the back, and either single or double-breasted. Younger men preferred the single-breasted look. Slacks were full and loose-fitting, and cuffs became popular. Trousers previously had been creased at the sides, but they now were creased front to back. Belts or suspenders held trousers in place. For the most part, suits were made of woolen fabric. Black, brown, dark blue, and gray were the colors of a mature man's suits, and they were the standard for business wear. During the late 1920s, younger men appeared in lighter, softer tones, often in tweed fabric. Well-to-do gentlemen shopped at Brooks Brothers, where a suit might cost $100 or more. Men of less affluence could purchase three-piece suits (jacket, trousers, and vest, or jacket with two pairs of pants) for $30 or less at their local department store.

In 1925, shirts changed from the detached-collar style to having attached collars. Detached collars had been made of starched white fabrics, celluloid, or more flexible three-ply cotton. They were replaced by one-piece shirts with collars in matched fabrics. Attached collars were button-down, plain-pointed, and pin-pointed (the points of the collar pinned under the tie). In addition to white shirts, men began wearing pastel blue, tan and yellow shirts. Some even wore pin-striped shirts. Ties, too, became more colorful, featuring stripes, plaids, and polka dots.

An unusual vogue in pants occurred on college campuses in 1925 when students began wearing "Oxford bags." Oxford bags were extremely full slacks that had originated at Britain's Oxford University in order for male students to cover their sporty knickers (short pants tucked at the knee), which were banned on campus. These wide-legged trousers often measured twenty-five inches at the knees and twenty-two inches at the cuffs. They were sewn from soft woolen flannel fabric and worn with sports jackets and bright-colored ties. Two sports jackets were popular during the decade: the navy blue woolen blazer with a crest on the left breast pocket, and the modified Norfolk tweed jacket with box pleats down each side and a belt at the back.

Campus outerwear was quite dapper during the decade. Students sported belted waterproof gabardine (a durable twill fabric of wool, rayon, or cotton) Burberry trench coats, just as British army officers had worn during World War I (1914–18). They also wore full-length camel-hair polo coats, knee-length velvet-lapelled chesterfield coats, and raccoon coats. On campus as well as in the business world, fashionable hats included the snap-brimmed fedora with a creased crown and the stiff round-topped derby. In summer, men favored stiff, round, flat-topped straw "boaters." For sports they wore soft woolen, cotton, or linen caps with short front brims.

Style-conscious men, particularly the younger crowd, were clean-shaven and wore their hair combed back and parted in the middle. Under-wear styles had started to change at the end of the previous decade from one-piece full-length union suits to thinner short one-piece garments with a drop seat, or more modern two-piece outfits consisting of an undershirt and loose shorts that featured a button-adjustable waist. During the decade, men began sleeping in pajamas in pastel solids or striped patterns instead of wearing nightshirts.

❖ SKYSCRAPERS DOMINATE URBAN LANDSCAPES

More than any other type of building, the skyscraper filled the bur-geoning business districts of cities across the nation during the 1920s. Commercial structures moved away from a style of ornate neo-gothic (a revival of the architecture style which had flourished in Europe from the twelfth through fifteenth centuries) of the previous decade to the clean, sleek Bauhaus school of design.

The Bauhaus was a popular German school of architecture founded by Walter Gropius (1883–1969) in 1919. Three years later the Bauhaus trend spread to America, spurred by a competition among architects to design the proposed Chicago Tribune Company building. The winning entry was the gothic-style drawing submitted by American architectural designers John Mead Howells (1868–1959) and Raymond M. Hood (1881–1934). Despite the winning choice, the bulk of the architectural world's attention went to the entry that received second prize. Finnish architect Eliel Saari-nen (1873–1950) stunned his colleagues with a proposal for a mountain-ous structure with setbacks at defined levels that eventually receded to a square unadorned peak. The Howell and Hood design was used to create the towering Tribune structure, which opened in 1925; however, Saari-nen's design was so impressive that even Hood stepped forward to praise its innovative plan. Encouraged by the praise and publicity, Saarinen moved to the United States in 1923 to design American buildings. His influence eventually helped to give a sleek and modern look to many of America's big cities.

Even so, the neo-gothic design with its buttresses (projecting wooden or masonry supports), spires and ornamentation, hearkening back to the Middle Ages, dominated commercial building design during the early years

*John Mead Howells and
Raymond M. Hood's
winning entry in a
competition among
architects was used to
create the towering
Chicago Tribune Company
building.* **Reproduced by
permission of the
Corbis Corporation.**

of the decade. From 1924 until late in the decade, the ziggurat (a pyramidal structure created by a series of setback blocks as the building attained height) provided the main design for business architecture. It emphasized a sense of power and understated adornment. At the end of the 1920s, commercial high-rises began taking on the look of a more slender, flat-roofed, horizontally defined slab that stressed function over ornamentation.

Certain changes in building design arose from legal necessity rather than from aesthetics. In New York City, a zoning law passed in 1916 limited the width of buildings in order to allow for air movement and admission of light onto the streets. That legislation brought in the trend of building pyramid-shaped towers that narrowed as they rose. Two skyscrapers that incorporated this ziggurat design were the New York Telephone Company Building (1926) and Raymond Hood's dramatic black American Radiator Building (1924), with its gold-gilded top and abstract gold-gilded decorations at setback points.

Saarinen's building designs were not the only foreign influence on American architecture and design in the 1920s. In July 1925, the Exposition Internationale des Arts Decoratifs and Industriels Modernes was held in Paris and proved to be a significant and influential exhibition of modern decorative style. The items on display showed a radical change from the older, gingerbread decoration of the Victorian style. From this event came the term "art deco." The art deco style of geometric shapes and simple lines would soon be integrated into such Manhattan landmarks as the Chrysler Building (1930) and the Empire State Building (1931). The popularity of art deco styling would carry through the 1930s.

❖ CITY RESIDENTS MOVE FROM TOWNHOUSES TO APARTMENT DWELLINGS

During the 1920s many people moved from rural homes, a trend that had begun during the previous decade. Individuals were drawn to the lively lifestyles of large urban centers where there were theaters, concerts, restaurants, speakeasies (night clubs that served illegal intoxicating liquor during the era of Prohibition), and the hope of obtaining a lucrative job. Certainly those aspects of city life were attractive; however, cities also spelled problems. Air and noise pollution, crime, and traffic congestion plagued big-city lifestyles. In Pittsburgh and Chicago, carbon monoxide in tunnels actually poisoned residents.

For affluent people, the trend in urban residences changed from one-family brownstones or townhouses to luxury apartment living. One reason for the conversion was the decrease in the number of people willing to work as in-home servants. By the late 1910s, the majority of servants had left their positions to make better wages in factories, retail stores, or offices. Without readily available household help, it no longer was practical to have a dining room that could accommodate one hundred diners. By the 1920s, wealthy people were buying large apartments in high-rise buildings, and they were building opulent weekend and summer mansions in adjacent suburbs or in the countryside.

In 1925, *Vanity Fair* magazine advertised ten- to fourteen-room (with four to five bathrooms) Manhattan cooperative high-rise apartments at

1020 Fifth Avenue for sale for $40,000 to $105,000 per unit. By contrast, less expensive New York City high-rise housing, mainly marketed to young professionals, could be purchased for $4,000 to $9,100, with 25 percent down and the remainder to be paid in monthly installments, plus a monthly operating charge from $37 to $85. Those specific prices represented the costs of apartments at Hudson View Gardens at 183rd Street and Pinehurst Avenue. Even though the majority of factory and office workers could not afford such apartments, for those who earned higher salaries the urban lifestyle could be quite luxurious and enjoyable.

❖ AMERICANS PAY ATTENTION TO INTERIOR DESIGN

More than in any previous decade, Americans of the 1920s were interested in interior design. In 1924, *Vanity Fair* magazine identified eight schools of interior design. Most were centered in New York City, with others in Boston and Cambridge, Massachusetts, and still others in San Francisco, California. Two movements had European branches in Paris, France; and Florence, Italy. Styles of interior decoration were named to reflect past eras such as (the reigns of) Louis XVI (Sixteenth) and Charles II, or American Colonial. Magazines such as *House Beautiful* and *Garden and Home* (later known as *Better Homes & Gardens*) catered to the new American pastime of interior decorating.

Conservative homes might be decorated with copies of eighteenth-century French furnishings, while trendy families might choose Art Moderne (a marriage of French art deco with German Bauhaus) decor. Surprisingly, the understated lines of the art deco and Bauhaus schools played only a small part in home furnishings until the very end of the decade. Instead, modernism in interior decoration meant choosing a period from the past and then adapting that choice to modern usage. The move to cloak modern design with period atmosphere was called historicism. Only the kitchen appliances appeared modern; the rest of the home was furnished with antiques, or more likely copies of older pieces. Modern radiators were covered in ornate grillwork, and electric lighting fixtures were styled to resemble candles and old-fashioned candelabras (branched candlesticks).

❖ FADS AND CRAZES IN A YOUTH-ORIENTED CULTURE

For many Americans, the 1920s was a time to expand interests and take time for recreation. While the war years had proven to be a period of sobriety and tension, the following decade provided a return to relaxed lifestyles and amusements. In this atmosphere, a number of games became popular and several frivolities captured the attention of many Americans, especially among the younger generation.

A Boom in Suburban Homelife

Millions of Americans were repelled by the bustle and pollution of large urban centers, but most wanted to remain near the recreational and cultural advantages of cities. For middle-class families, city life was not only crowded and hectic, but it also was too expensive. For those folks, a home in the suburbs was the key to contentment. During the 1920s, the housing industry was booming. In 1922 alone, 767,000 units were constructed, and 1,048,000 homes were built in 1925. Most of the new homes were located in expanding suburban communities.

Originally, suburbs such as Grosse Pointe, Michigan; Lake Forest, Illinois; and Tuxedo Park, New York were constructed as country getaways for wealthy city dwellers. By the start of the 1920s, a small family with an annual income of $2,500 could purchase a house in the suburbs by making most of the payments in monthly installments. In 1920, attractive bungalow homes could be purchased for $3,000 to $10,000.

Families with lower incomes could purchase prefabricated houses. A prospective homeowner could buy all the necessary materials in a package but would need handyman skills to put the structure together. In 1923, the Aladdin Company advertised plans, precut lumber, and hardware for a simple five-room house for $538. Their twelve-room Dutch Colonial home cost $1,932. Despite the inexpensive price tags, prefabricated residences never became a hit with Americans.

Crossword puzzles became a widespread craze after the world's first collection *The Cross Word Puzzle Book* was published in 1924 by Richard Leo Simon (1899–1960) and Max Lincoln Schuster (1897–1970). Simon and Schuster were so concerned that the book would fail to sell that they published it under a separate imprint, rather than under the name of their own well-known publishing company. With a pencil attached to each volume, the book became a best-seller. Crossword puzzles became a nationwide rage. Newspapers began publishing crossword puzzles, and the University of Kentucky even offered a course in crosswords as "educational, scientific, instructive and mentally stimulative as well as entertaining."

Another diversion that became a national pastime was the traditional Chinese game of mah-jongg, introduced in the United States in 1922.

Women, in particular, formed mah-jongg clubs, but the game also intrigued many college students in dormitories and fraternities. Playing mah-jongg required a set of 144 carved tiles made of ivory, bone, celluloid, or later plastic. The game's constantly changing rules for what constitutes a winning hand called for frequently publishing new guidelines. More than twenty rule books were published during the decade.

Flagpole-sitting may have been the most ridiculous fad of the decade. A flagpole sitter would balance while seated on a small disc atop a flagpole with stirrups for bracing oneself. He or she would take a five-minute nap each hour. A champion flagpole sitter might stay aloft for days or even weeks!

Dance marathons consisted of couples dancing for days on end until only one couple remained on the dance floor. Young couples struggled to keep their feet moving while they watched the competition collapse around them. In 1928, ninety-one couples danced in a marathon that lasted nearly three weeks—482 hours—in the hopes of winning a $5,000 prize.

One youthful craze that was frowned upon by parents was petting parties. During the 1920s teenagers formed a new type of peer culture. They went to school together where they formed attachments and socialized after school by going to movies or riding unsupervised in automobiles. Boy/girl relationships arose, leading to necking and petting without a commitment of marriage. The new range of behavior in social encounters for high school students, without actual sexual intercourse, proved quite a change from old-fashioned chaperoned dances.

❖ THE BIRTH CONTROL MOVEMENT

In the 1920s women in all economic brackets gained greater ability to limit the number of their pregnancies. This new freedom of choice was due to the dedicated work of women's rights advocate and nurse Margaret Sanger (1883–1966). In 1921, Sanger organized the American Birth Control League, which became the Planned Parenthood Federation in 1942. In 1923, she opened the Birth Control Clinical Research Bureau in New York City. Sanger spoke out against false claims that birth control devices, such as diaphragms, were obscene.

❖ THE RISE AND RETREAT OF RELIGIOUS FUNDAMENTALISM

One of the most dynamic conflicts in organized religion during the 1920s arose between fundamentalist and modernist Protestants. During the early years of the decade, fundamentalists controlled much of the American Protestant church and, indirectly, many phases of American culture. By the end of the decade, the modernists had taken over the Protestant church.

Families consisted of fewer children during the 1920s. In 1900, the average number of children born to a woman who lived the usual number of childbearing years was 3.56. In 1920, that figure dropped to 3.17, and further decreased to 2.5 in 1925. By 1935, the average was 1.8 children per child-bearing woman.

These changes meant that adults could pay more attention to each child. Since families did not send their children to work as frequently as they had earlier in the century, youngsters were considered economically useless but emotionally priceless. Yet many middle-class parents followed the strict child-rearing teachings of psychiatrist John B. Watson (1878–1958), the founder of behaviorism. This "scientific" approach, which prevailed in many homes until the 1940s, involved limiting the show of affection and enforcing a strict regimen of habit training in feeding, toilet training, and discipline.

One contemporary issue that split the Protestant church in the decade was Darwinism, or the theory of evolution. The idea that species could evolve based on concepts of survival of the fittest clashed with the fundamentalist concept that the human race emerged from Adam and Eve, as created by God. This issue was brought to the public's attention through the much-publicized Scopes Monkey Trial of 1925, during which John T. Scopes (1900–1970), a biology teacher in Tennessee, was accused of breaking a new state law by teaching evolution. After the trial, many Americans came to see the anti-evolution fundamentalist viewpoint as ignorant and unsophisticated.

In addition, the prohibition of manufacturing, selling, and transporting intoxicating liquor, set into law by the ratification of the Eighteenth Amendment in 1920, became a very unpopular restriction for many Americans. A good number of anti-Prohibitionists blamed the passage of the amendment on conservative Protestant fundamentalists, which damaged the popularity of their opinions even further.

❖ RELIGION AND POPULAR CULTURE

As movie attendance and riding in automobiles began filling weekend time, church attendance declined. As a result, religious leaders, journalists, and radio broadcasters who dealt with topics of religion started to wage campaigns against popular culture. They especially disliked Hollywood films that featured love affairs, crime, and other "immoral" activities.

Early in the decade, motion picture stars became involved in two notorious scandals that gave moralists ammunition against movie-going. The first scandal focused on the trial of silent film comedy star Roscoe "Fatty" Arbuckle (1887–1933), who was accused of raping a young woman at a "wild party." Arbuckle was acquitted, but months of headlines about the immorality of Hollywood stars led the conservative public to develop a general distrust of Hollywood film folks. The second scandal revolved around the murder of Hollywood director William Desmond Taylor (1877–1922). Suspects included film stars, and the evidence linked Taylor to drugs and illicit love affairs.

To tame Hollywood's apparent recklessness, movie executives, who feared a loss of box office revenue, agreed to bring in a committee to ensure the morality of the movies. Presbyterian elder Will Hays (1879–1954) was chosen in 1922 to head the Motion Picture Producers and Distributors of America, Inc. (MPPDA) to improve the image of the Hollywood community and otherwise "clean up" the movies seen by millions of American families.

For More Information

BOOKS

Allen, Frederick Lewis. *America Transforms Itself: 1900–1950*. New Brunswick, NJ: Transaction Pub., 1993.

Allen, Frederick Lewis. *Only Yesterday: An Informal History of the 1920s*. New York: Perennial Classics, 2000.

Altman, Linda Jacobs. *The Decade That Roared: America During Prohibition*. New York: Twenty-First Century books, 1997.

Bachrach, Deborah. *The Importance of Margaret Sanger*. San Diego: Lucent Books, 1993.

Bolden, Tonya, ed. *33 Things Every Girl Should Know About Women's History: From Suffragettes to Skirt Lengths to the E.R.A.* New York: Crown Publishing, 2002.

Feinstein, Stephen. *The 1920s: From Prohibition to Charles Lindbergh*. Berkeley Heights, NJ: Enslow Publishers, 2001.

Herald, Jacqueline. *Fashions of a Decade: The 1920s*. New York: Facts on File, 1991.

Hintz, Martin. *Farewell, John Barleycorn: Prohibition in the United States*. Minneapolis: Lerner Publications, 1996.

Lucas, Eileen. *The Eighteenth and Twenty-First Amendments: Alcohol—Prohibition and Repeal.* Springfield, NJ: Enslow Publishers, 1998.

Matuz, Roger. *Albert Kahn: Architect of Detroit.* Detroit: Wayne State University Press, 2001.

Pietrusza, David. *The Roaring Twenties.* San Diego: Lucent Books, 1998.

Ruby, Jennifer. *Costume in Context: The 1920s and 1930s.* London: B.T. Batsford, Ltd, 1988.

Severance, John B. *Skyscrapers: How America Grew Up.* New York: Holiday House, 2000.

Stefoff, Rebecca. *Charles Darwin and the Evolution Revolution.* New York: Oxford University Press, 1996.

Topalian, Elyse. *Margaret Sanger.* New York: Franklin Watts, 1984.

Wallis, Jeremy. *Coco Chanel.* Chicago: Heinemann Library, 2002.

Whitelaw, Nancy. *Margaret Sanger: Every Child a Wanted Child.* New York: Dillon Press, 1994.

WEB SITES

Media History Timeline: 1920s. http://www.mediahistory.umn.edu/time/1920s.html (accessed on August 5, 2002).

1920s. http://www.richland2.org/svh/Media/socstud/1920s.htm (accessed on August 5, 2002).

1920s. http://www.usgennet.org/usa/il/state/alhn1920.html (accessed on August 5, 2002).

Medicine and Health

1920: The Menninger Clinic, which specialized in treating individuals with mental health afflictions, opens in Topeka, Kansas.

1920: Phenobarbital is introduced as a treatment for epilepsy.

1920: Researchers discover that cancer removes 35 percent of the oxygen from the human cells.

1921: Carl Jung publishes *Psychological Types*, in which he offers his views on such innovative concepts as introverted and extroverted personality traits.

1921: Marie Stopes opens the first family planning clinic in London.

1922: The U.S. Federal Narcotics Control Board is established. It is empowered to ban the importation of nonmedicinal narcotics.

1922: It is reported that more than one hundred radiologists have died from X-ray-induced cancer.

1922: Frederick Hopkins discovers glutathione, a sequence of three amino acids that are essential for the utilization of oxygen by a cell.

1922: Joseph Erlanger and Herbert Gasser use an oscilloscope to study electrical impulses in a single nerve fiber.

1922: Samuel Torrey Orton announces completion of a study in which he links emotional disturbances to neurological disorders.

1922: *The Sex Side of Life,* a family planning pamphlet, is declared obscene, and cannot be mailed in the United States.

1923: The first birth control clinic opens in New York City under the direction of Margaret Sanger.

1924: Seale Harris discovers that sugar can cause hyperinsulinism (a condition resulting from excessive secretions of insulin in the body). He determines that diets should include decreased amounts of sugar.

1924: Theodor Svedberg invents the ultra-centrifuge, a high-speed machine that makes it possible to isolate viruses.

1924: Rudolph Matas introduces the use of an intravenous saline solution to prevent dehydration.

1924: Heroin is outlawed in the United States as a prescription drug.

1924: Acetylene, a colorless, gaseous hydrocarbon (an organic compound made up of hydrogen and carbon) is used as an anesthetic.

1924: Faulty diphtheria vaccinations result in the deaths of forty-five people in Connecticut and New Hampshire.

1925: James B. Collip discovers parathormone, a hormone secreted by the parathyroid gland.

1925: February 2 A husky named Balto leads a team of sled dogs across 650 miles of snowy terrain, carrying diphtheria medicine which saves countless lives in Nome, Alaska.

1925: June At an international arms control and trade convention in Geneva, Switzerland, nations unite to ban the use of bacteriological and chemical weapons in wartime.

1926: Spiroptera carcinoma, a cancer caused by a parasite, is discovered.

1926: A chemical, later identified as acetylcholine, is shown to be involved in the transmission of nerve impulses.

1926: The General Medical Society for Psychotherapy, an international organization, is created in Germany.

1926: E. L. Thorndike publishes *The Measurement of Intelligence,* in which he describes how intelligence may be numerically calculated.

1926: James B. Sumner isolates and crystallizes urease, an enzyme.

1927: The first tetanus shots are administered to humans in France.

1927: The League of Nations sponsors a conference in The Hague, Netherlands, to explore the reasons behind a rash of vaccination-induced deaths in Europe.

1928: At the Third International Conference for Eugenics, one participant calls for the sterilization of 14 million Americans with low IQs.

1928: Research shows that prolactin, a pituitary hormone, causes the production of milk in breasts.

1929: Alexander Fleming reports his discovery of penicillin.

1929: Edward Doisy discovers theelin, a female sex hormone, in the urine of pregnant women.

1929: Adolph Butenandt determines the chemical structure of estrone, a female sex hormone.

1929: Manfred J. Sakel uses insulin shock as a treatment for schizophrenia.

1929: Jean Piaget proposes his theory of developmental psychology, in which he explains how individuals acquire knowledge.

Overview

During the 1920s, great strides were made in ridding the world of such communicable, and potentially deadly, diseases as tuberculosis, measles, scarlet fever, and syphilis. Medical pioneers discovered and perfected a range of new instruments which aided doctors in diagnosing and treating illness. Among them were the electroencephalograph, which measured brain waves; the Papanicolaou (or "Pap") smear, which aided in the early detection of cancer; and the iron lung, which assisted individuals who were unable to breathe on their own. Reuben Leon Kahn introduced a more accurate blood test for syphilis, which replaced the one devised by Albert Wassermann in 1906. One of the decade's great discoveries was that the consumption of calves' liver was an effective cure for anemia, an iron deficiency in the blood. Another was that insulin, produced in the pancreas, effectively controls diabetes. Until that time, diabetes was a fatal disease. Other medical breakthroughs, however, were embraced by some, but not all. One controversial medical technique was the Rorschach (or inkblot) test, which allowed psychiatrists to evaluate the mental processes of patients.

Those whose medical and health-related innovations came during previous decades were honored in the 1920s for their earlier achievements. For example, Willem Einthoven, the discoverer of the electrocardiograph, which measures electrical currents in the heart, won the Nobel

Prize for physiology or medicine in 1924. Five years later, Christiaan Eijkman and Frederick Hopkins shared the same Nobel Prize for discovering vitamin A and determining that vitamins are necessary to maintain good health. Meanwhile, initial findings were made during the 1920s which led to groundbreaking medical advances in future decades. One major breakthrough was the accidental discovery of penicillin, an antibiotic fungus, by Alexander Fleming in 1928. Two decades later, penicillin could be artificially produced and became the world's most effective life-saving drug.

Much headway was made in combating such rampant diseases as hookworm and pellagra, which primarily plagued individuals residing in rural areas. During the decade, vitamins B[1], C, D, E, and K were isolated or discovered. Theories were put forth regarding the nature of personality traits and the numerical measurement of intelligence. Advances were made in the areas of women's and children's health. At the beginning of the 1920s, infant mortality and maternity death rates were alarmingly high. The Sheppard-Towner Maternity and Infancy Protection Act, passed by the U.S. Congress in 1921, made funding available for health care clinics and educational materials for pregnant women and mothers. Unfortunately, pressure on the part of political conservatives and the American Medical Association (AMA) led to the act's repeal before the decade ended. Meanwhile, birth control advocates organized conferences and opened clinics; they also met with resistance from those who were antifamily planning.

Harvey Williams Cushing (1869–1939) During World War I (1914–18), Harvey Williams Cushing, a brain surgeon, organized a medical unit that operated on soldiers who had received brain injuries in battle. He later wrote an authoritative paper on wartime brain impairment. During the 1920s, he frequently published books and articles on different facets of brain surgery. One of his prime contributions was a paper on intracranial tumors; Cushing identified a condition in which muscular weakness and obesity results from excessive production of ACTH, a protein hormone, secreted by the pituitary gland. The syndrome came to be known as Cushing's disease. *Photo reproduced by courtesy of the Library of Congress.*

George (1881–1967) and Gladys (1881–1963) Dick Working at the McCormick Institute of Infectious Diseases in Chicago, the husband-and-wife team of George and Gladys Dick created a diagnostic test to determine a patient's vulnerability to scarlet fever, a deadly disease that had taken countless lives. Eventually, they were able to identify streptococcus (a bacteria) in the throats of scarlet fever patients and demonstrate that strep was the cause of the disease. The scarlet fever test that emerged from their research is named the "Dick test," after its discoverers.

Abraham Flexner (1866–1959) Abraham Flexner was noted for his efforts as a medical educator and reformer. Early in the century, he authored a groundbreaking report in which he criticized medical schools for placing profit and self-interest ahead of learning. In the report, he advised that 120 of the 155 medical schools in existence in the United States and Canada be closed. During the 1920s, he published several important reports on the status of medical education. *Photo reproduced courtesy of the Library of Congress.*

Simon Flexner (1863–1946) Simon Flexner, brother of Abraham Flexner, was a researcher in the fields of pathology (the study of the nature of diseases) and bacteriology (the science that relates to bacteria). Among his many accomplishments were the isolation of a strain of dysentery; the injection of serum into the spinal canal, resulting in a reduction in the death rate from meningitis; and research which laid the groundwork for the development of a polio vaccine. As a member of the scientific board of directors of the Rockefeller Institute for Medical Research, he divided the organization into departments which centered on specific areas of medical research. In 1924, he was named the institute's director.

Reuben Leon Kahn (1887–1974) Reuben Leon Kahn's achievements as a medical researcher transcended his development of the test that became the standard for detecting syphilis. This discovery was just a stepping stone in his examination of the role that different tissues play in immunizing the body from a host of diseases. His specialty was serology (the science that deals with the properties and reactions of serums), and Kahn authored over 170 publications that dealt with the potential impact of serums as fighters against disease.

Karl Landsteiner (1868–1943) Karl Landsteiner's overriding scientific achievement was the transformation of serology from an accumulation of seemingly unrelated phenomena into a division of chemical science. He researched such diseases as polio and syphilis, transmitting the former and producing the latter in animals. Among his most far-reaching discoveries was the existence of different blood types, which elevated the safety of blood transfusions and made surgery a safer procedure. He and his colleagues discovered what came to be known as the Rh factor (genetically determined substances present in the red blood cells of 85 percent of all human beings). *Photo reproduced courtesy of the Library of Congress.*

Thomas Milton Rivers (1888–1962) Thomas Milton Rivers was famous for his exploration in the area of viral diseases. After years of research, he announced in 1926 a controversial theory which distinguished between bacteria and viruses. Unlike most bacteria, according to Rivers, the manner in which viruses reproduce depends upon living cells in the host (the living being that initially sustains the virus). Despite the protests of his skeptical colleagues, Rivers's theory proved to be true, and it established virology as a separate area of study for those wishing to research the causes of disease.

George Hoyt Whipple (1878–1978) George Hoyt Whipple's principal interest was the research of blood and liver ailments. His experiments proved that the consumption of calves' liver eased the effects of anemia, a malady in which the blood is lacking hemoglobin (an iron-containing protein found in red blood cells). While at the University of Rochester in 1921, his experiments with laboratory dogs proved that diets rich in liver combated anemia. His findings were announced four years later, and soon thereafter a liver extract was commercially marketed. Then in 1926, physicians George Richards Minot (1885–1950) and William Parry Murphy (1892–1987) developed a liver-based treatment for pernicious (severe) anemia, which then was a fatal disease.

◆ *Topics in the News* ....

❖ **COMMUNICABLE DISEASES: RIDDING THE WORLD OF DEADLY INFECTION**

During the 1920s, individuals who contracted a host of diseases found their health seriously imperiled and their lives endangered. Back then, measles was a common childhood illness. Its symptoms include fever, sore throat, and skin rash. While the disease usually was not fatal if the child who contracted it received adequate care, large percentages of youngsters in foundling hospitals died of measles during the decade. Additionally, a very real danger existed for developing blindness. One of the initial steps in finding a cure for measles was the identification and isolation of the microorganism (germ) that caused the disease. While this was not accomplished during the decade, a measles-fighting serum was developed from the blood of convalescing measles patients; it provided limited resistance to the disease.

Prior to 1923, scarlet fever was a menace to the health and well-being of people of all ages. Those who contracted this deadly contagious disease were in danger of suffering from blindness, deafness, heart and kidney ailments, and permanent paralysis. Usually a yellow flag and a printed notice were posted outside the home of an afflicted individual to warn potential visitors of the danger. A person with scarlet fever usually remained isolated for one month, after which the room in which he or she resided had to be fumigated. Clothing and dishes used by the infected individual had to be carefully cleaned with disinfectant.

Among the symptoms of scarlet fever are a red body rash and inflammation of the mouth, throat, and nose. Early in the decade, husband-and-wife researchers George (1881–1967) and Gladys (1881–1963) Dick isolated the germ that caused scarlet fever. Their effort led to the development in 1924 of a serum that effectively battled the disease. While this serum eliminated the potential of mass epidemics of scarlet fever, there still was no cure.

Tuberculosis was another lethal communicable disease common in the 1920s. It was caused by the presence of bacteria in the body; while it could ravage just about any organ or tissue, well over 90 percent of all tuberculosis cases were centered in the lungs. Before the decade began, researchers were able to identify carriers of the disease. Then in 1921, French microbiologist Albert Calmette (1863–1933) and veterinarian Camille Guerin (1872–1961) produced the first tuberculosis vaccine. This breakthrough resulted from their discovery that the body's immune system built up a resistance to the disease after being exposed to a mild tuberculosis infection. Calmette and Guerin's vaccine, known as the BCG (Bacillus Calmette-

Guerin), first was used in Paris in 1922. By the end of the decade, it was employed throughout Europe and Asia. However, the medical community in England and the United States demanded more extensive testing. It was not until the 1950s that the vaccine was accepted worldwide.

Syphilis, a disease that is caused primarily by sexual contact, can be fatal if left untreated. Side effects include paralysis and mental derangement. In 1906, August von Wasserman (1866–1925), a German bacteriologist, devised the first syphilis test. It involved examining the blood of the infected individual to see if antibodies had formed within the body to fight the disease. Not only was the Wasserman test complicated and time-consuming, but its overall effectiveness was also questioned. The February 1923 issue of the *American Journal of Public Health* noted that the "many variable elements of this test give it numerous sources of error.... " Reuben Leon Kahn (1887–1979), a major in the U.S. Army Medical Service Corps (MSC), had developed a blood test that was easier, quicker, and far more accurate. Kahn introduced his test in 1923; soon afterwards, his method was used regularly around the world.

❖ DIAGNOSIS TECHNOLOGY: GETTING TO THE ROOT OF DISEASE

During the 1920s, a host of newly developed instruments enabled doctors to chart the functions of the body and diagnose illnesses more easily. Hans Berger (1873–1941), a German psychiatrist and scientist, was fascinated by the function of the brain and the relationship between the brain and the mind. Understanding this connection, he believed, would provide insight into mental functioning and disturbances. His attempts to discover a method of detecting and recording human brain waves resulted in his invention of the electroencephalograph, which employs a pair of electrodes (electric conductors) placed on the scalp to transmit the wave patterns to one of the instrument's several recording channels. Berger made his first unsuccessful attempt to record brain waves in 1920 by stimulating the cortex (the outer layer of the cerebrum and cerebellum, which are two parts of the brain) of individuals suffering from skull defects. He did so by applying electrical current to the skin covering the defect. Despite his failure, Berger carried on his work. Before the end of the decade, he had devised his electroencephalograph and successfully recorded the first electroencephalogram (more commonly known as an EEG). EEGs became a vital source of information for doctors examining patients who had suffered significant head injuries, cerebral infections, brain tumors, and illnesses related to the nervous system. For his work, Berger earned recognition as the "father of electroencephalography."

George N. Papanicolaou (1883–1962), a Greek physician who settled in the United States in 1913, specialized in cytology (the area of biology that centers on the make-up, function, history, and production within the body of cells). Upon studying the vaginal discharges of female guinea pigs, Papanicolaou observed changes in the sizes and shapes of their cells. He associated these changes with alterations in the uterus and ovaries that occurred during the pig's menstrual cycle. He identified similar changes in the vaginal cells of women, and he noted abnormalities in the cells of those patients afflicted with cervical cancer. All this research resulted in his perfecting what came to be known as the Papanicolaou (or "Pap") smear: a procedure in which cells are subjected to a staining (coloring) technique that marks diseased tissue. The "Pap" smear proved an invaluable tool in early cancer detection. It enabled doctors to note the presence of cancer cells five to ten years prior to the appearance of symptoms. Besides cervical cancer, the test was employed in the diagnosis of colon, prostate, bladder, lung, breast, sinus, and kidney cancer. Papanicolaou began his research in 1920. He first announced his findings eight years later, in a paper titled "New Cancer Diagnosis." At the time, he noted that "a better understanding and more accurate analysis of the cancer problem is bound to result from use of this method." However, "Pap" smears were not widely accepted until the late 1940s.

Some medical devices had been developed in previous decades; during the 1920s, their inventors were honored for their work. In 1887, Augustus Waller (1856–1922), a lecturer at St. Mary's Medical School in London, demonstrated the possibility of measuring heart activity. In 1903, Willem Einthoven (1860–1927), a Dutch physiologist, expanded on Waller's work. He developed the first practical electrocardiograph, a machine which measured electrical currents of the heart and diagnosed irregularities in heart action. Einthoven's first machine was a string galvanometer (a device which consists of a thin thread on which the electrical current is detected and measured). He continued perfecting the process; eventually, electrodes attached to wires were placed on the patient, whose heartbeat was recorded. The electrocardiograph became an important diagnostic resource for patients with heart ailments. For his work, Einthoven was awarded the Nobel Prize for physiology or medicine in 1924.

❖ HEALTH OF WOMEN AND CHILDREN: SIGNIFICANT REFORMS AND BACKLASH

In 1921, approximately eighteen thousand American women died during childbirth. Meanwhile, the previous year, 248,432 American children under the age of five had died. The death rate for infants in orphanages approached 100 percent.

In 1946, Dr. Benjamin Spock (1903–1998) published his *Common Sense Book of Baby and Child Care,* a landmark guide that became the preeminent source for sound advice on child rearing. The earlier decades of the century also had their own primary authority on babies: Dr. L. Emmett Holt (1855–1924), a professor of pediatrics at Columbia University. In 1894, Holt first published his influential book, *The Care and Feeding of Children.* Through 1935, it was updated and republished fourteen times. His advice was archaic when compared to Spock's. Contemporary parents who followed it might even be accused of child neglect!

Holt theorized that mothers should not pick up crying babies because they would become spoiled if overly handled. He wrote, "Babies under six months old should never be played with; and the less of it at any time the better for the infant." He even recommended that babies wear mittens or have their hands fastened to their sides during sleep, to prevent sucking and masturbation. "In more obstinate cases," he suggested, "it may be necessary to confine the elbow by small pasteboard splints...."

These figures were startling and disturbing. The harsh reality that childbirth was a potentially deadly proposition and that youngsters were susceptible to a range of possibly fatal maladies resulted in swift government action. Child hygiene information was made available to parents. Public health and infant welfare services were established. Six national health groups united to form the American Child Health Organization. Its president was Herbert Hoover (1874–1964), who in 1928 was elected U.S. president. During the 1920s, Hoover helped raise funds to support health education in America's schools and supported immunization against diphtheria and smallpox. He even headed a fund drive that netted the American Red Cross $15 million in donations.

The Sheppard-Towner Maternity and Infancy Protection Act, passed by the U.S. Congress in 1921, was a milestone in health reform for women and children. Sheppard-Towner grew out of women's concerns for their children's health, and their very real fears that their offspring would die. The cause of high infant mortality rates during the 1920s was not so much a lack of scientific knowledge as a lack of education and available health services for women. The act made available federal funding for prenatal (prebirth) and infant health clinics and educational material for pregnant women and mothers. It was operated by the Children's Bureau, a division of the U.S. Department of Labor.

Initially, Sheppard-Towner was to remain in effect for five years. During this period, the infant mortality rate significantly declined, while the maternal death rate also moved downward. However, when the law came up for renewal in 1926, political conservatives denounced the program's female administrators as socialists. The American Medical Association (AMA) also lobbied for the repeal of Sheppard-Towner, because its members reportedly dreaded the competition presented by free health centers. Even though the act was supported by President Calvin Coolidge (1872–1933), it only remained in place for another two years before being repealed. Between 1928 and 1932, fourteen attempts were made to reverse the repeal. All of them failed.

❖ INSULIN: COMMUTING A DEATH SENTENCE

Diabetes, a disease that often occurs in children, is an ailment in which the pancreas is unable to produce the proper level of insulin. Insulin is essential for muscle cells to utilize glucose (the form of sugar absorbed into the body). Each year, diabetes killed untold thousands. Before the 1920s, a diabetes diagnosis was considered the equivalent of a death sentence.

During the early 1900s, countless diabetes-related experiments were conducted. Finally, Frederick Grant Banting (1891–1941), a young Canadian physician, began experimenting with the assistance of Charles Best (1899–1978), a twenty-one-year-old medical student. The two worked in a laboratory at the University of Toronto where John J.R. MacLeod (1876–1935), a professor of physiology and head of the school's physiology department, was an authority in diabetes research. MacLeod initially was skeptical about Banting and Best's desire to conduct research. In May 1921, after MacLeod went on holiday to his native Scotland, Banting and Best took over one of the university's laboratories. Within months, they were able to induce a diabetic coma in a dog by removing its pancreas. Then they restored the animal to health with a substance they had isolated from the pancreas of another dog. They labeled this substance the "X Factor." However, the first animal soon died. This led Banting and Best to determine that the "X Factor" needed to be injected into the diabetes sufferer each day. The two conducted further experiments, and eventually they named the "X Factor" insulin.

The following year, Banting and Best tested insulin on themselves to prove that it was not harmful. Then they injected it into a twelve-year-old boy who was dying of diabetes. He quickly recovered. Other sufferers soon came forward, and soon insulin was being administered to countless diabetics. While Banting and Best labored to determine how to produce mass quantities of insulin, MacLeod traveled around offering lectures on "his" discovery.

Banting's life had been touched by diabetes: when he was fifteen, both his best friend and his sweetheart succumbed to the disease. Meanwhile, Best's favorite aunt recently had died of diabetes. As a result, both men were determined to find a cure for the disease. While insulin intake does not cure diabetes, it provides a way of effectively controlling the disease, and its discovery has prolonged the lives of millions. In 1923, Banting and MacLeod were awarded the Nobel Prize for physiology or medicine as "co-discoverers" of insulin. Banting believed that Best also should have been acknowledged, and gave half of his monetary prize to his colleague. MacLeod then agreed to share half of his prize with James B. Collip (1892–1965), the chemist who had worked with them to purify the "X Factor."

❖ NEW MEDICAL MACHINERY: THE IRON LUNG

During the 1920s, polio (poliomyelitis, or infantile paralysis) was still an infectious and deadly disease. Sufferers were afflicted with nerve cell destruction, muscle deterioration, and crippled limbs. The invention of the iron lung, a mechanical respirator, greatly eased the plight of polio victims, and allowed them to stay alive indefinitely. The lung was devised by Philip Drinker (1894–1972) of Harvard University after he observed research into the development of artificial respiration techniques for patients who had just undergone surgery. Drinker and his colleagues experimented using paralyzed cats. The iron lung they developed consisted of a large, airtight metal tank into which all but the head of the patient was placed. The machine breathed for the patient by operating a set of bellows (an instrument which draws in and discharges air). The bellows created pressure inside the machine, which acted like a human diaphragm and freed the patient's lung to expand and contract. The iron lung was first used in 1928 on an eight-year-old polio sufferer who was experiencing respiratory paralysis. The machine kept her breathing for five days, until she died of other polio-related complications. Next it was used on a Harvard student afflicted with polio. The lung assisted him in his breathing for several weeks. Eventually, he recovered.

For several decades, the iron lung remained an indispensable tool for saving the lives of polio patients. It was not until the 1950s that the development of a polio vaccine effectively eliminated the disease.

Medical Nonmiracles

In 1927, Morris Fishbein (1889–1976), editor of the *Journal of the American Medical Association,* published a book with lengthy, unusual, and self-explanatory title: *The New Medical Follies: An Encyclopedia of Cultism and Quackery in These United States, with Essays on The Cult of Beauty, The Craze of Reduction, Rejuvenation, Eclecticism, Bread and Dietary Fads, Physical Therapy, and a Forecast as to the Physician of the Future.*

Fishbein wrote,

> Among the hundred or more types of healing offered to the sophisticated is aerotherapy. Obviously aerotherapy means treatment by air, but in this instance hot air is particularly concerned. The patient is baked in a hot oven. Heat relieves pain and produces an increased flow of blood to the part heated.... Aerotherapy as one department of physical therapy becomes a cult when it is used to the exclusion of all other forms of healing. In New York a progressive quack established an institute equipped with special devices for pouring hot air over various portions of the body. He issued a beautiful brochure, illustrated with the likenesses of beautiful damsels in various states of negligee, smiling the smile of the satisfied.... In this document appeared incidentally the claim that hot air will cure anything from ague to zoster....

Fishbein also observed,

> One Dr. Fitzgerald of Hartford, Connecticut, has divided the body into zones, lengthwise and crosswise, and heals disease in one zone by pressing of others. To keep the pressure going he developed little wire springs. For instance, a toothache on the right side may be 'cured' by fastening a little spring around the second toe on the left foot. Naturally, Fitzgerald has never convinced any one with ordinary reasoning powers that there is anything to his system—except what he gets out of it.

❖ PENICILLIN: THE ORIGINS OF A LIFESAVING DRUG

Some health-related breakthroughs made during the 1920s laid the groundwork for future scientific innovations. One was the discovery of penicillin by Alexander Fleming (1881–1955), a Scottish bacteriologist and research scientist.

Early in the decade, Fleming discovered lysozyme, an antibacterial substance found in such body fluids as mucus, saliva, and tears. Then in

A Rorschach ink blot. Hermann Rorschach devised the test whereby patients would be shown a series of ten symmetrical ink blots and describe what they "saw" within the patterns. As a result, aspects of the patients' personalities were revealed. **Reproduced by permission of Photo Researchers, Inc.**

1928, he was organizing some petri dishes in which he had been growing bacteria. Fleming noticed that mold was growing on one of the dishes. He further observed that the mold had killed the bacteria. After taking a sample of the mold, he found that it was from the penicillium family. He named its active ingredient penicillin and first reported his discovery the following year. Fleming continued experimenting with the mold, while chemists began to grow and refine it. In 1950, penicillin was produced artificially for the first time. This breakthrough, directly linked to Fleming's 1928 discovery, resulted in the widespread employment of penicillin as an infection-fighting agent and the world's most effective lifesaving drug.

❖ RORSCHACH TEST: HIDDEN PSYCHOLOGICAL MEANINGS

In 1921 Hermann Rorschach (1884–1922), a Swiss psychoanalyst, devised a test whereby patients undergoing mental evaluation would be shown a series of ten symmetrical ink blots. Upon observing them, patients described and interpreted what they "saw" within the patterns, details, and shadings. As a result, aspects of their personality were revealed.

While previously, psychiatrists had employed such tests as free-association exercises, Rorschach believed that a carefully devised examination could be used as a major component in offering a thorough psychological evaluation of a patient. According to Rorschach, descriptions and responses could be analyzed to determine the psychological processes existing within the patient's mind. This data would then allow the psychiatrist to diagnose specific clinical disorders.

During subsequent decades, scientists have questioned the value of the Rorschach test. However, it has been extensively used in many countries around the world.

❖ RURAL DISEASES: HOOKWORM, PELLAGRA, AND TULAREMIA

A number of serious diseases primarily plagued residents of America's hinterlands. Before and during the early years of the twentieth century, many of those living in the rural South were impoverished and wore no shoes. As a result, they were susceptible to hookworm, a disease that manifested itself in warm climates. The worm that caused the malady was hatched from the larvae of eggs found in soil tainted by human excrement. After entering the body through the feet, the worm made its way into the victim's intestinal tract. From there, it lived off the victim's blood.

The hookworm-infected individual suffered from anemia and often died. Afflicted youngsters, if they survived, often emerged with physical and mental deficiencies. To combat hookworm, the Rockefeller Foundation organized a health commission to inform people about proper sanitation. Between 1910 and 1915, the foundation surveyed sixteen southern counties and determined that the rate of hookworm infection was 59.2 percent. By 1923, the rate had decreased to 23.9 percent. Nonetheless, hookworm remained a serious problem in America throughout the decade.

Pellagra was an often fatal malady with symptoms including skin rashes, stomach irregularities, and mental disorders. At the beginning of the 1910s, its cause and cure remained unknown. Joseph Goldberger (1874–1929), a U.S. Public Health Service (USPHS) researcher, was assigned to study the disease. Goldberger determined that pellagra was caused by improper nutrition and could be abated by adding protein and niacin to the diet. He also found that brewer's yeast was an effective remedy. In 1927, the USPHS determined that 170,000 Americans were afflicted with pellagra; from 1924 through 1928, the mortality rate was 58 percent. For six years, beginning in 1927, the American Red Cross handed out over two hundred thousand pounds of brewer's yeast in an effort to combat the disease.

Tularemia, a lesser-known affliction, was as equally jarring to its sufferers. This communicable disease was caused by an organism that grew in the blood of infected rodents, and its symptoms included fever, body-aches, headache, chills, vomiting, sore and oversized lymph glands, and a circular sore at the location of the infection. Those most at risk included anyone who spent large amounts of time outdoors; victims included hunters and butchers who had handled infected meat, or any individual bitten by a tick or deer fly that previously had bitten an infected animal. During the 1920s, treatment for tularemia primarily consisted of lengthy bed rest, lasting between two months and a year. In later decades, such antibiotics (chemical substances, produced by microorganisms, that halt the growth of or completely destroy bacteria) as streptomycin, gentamycin, and tobramycin were used to combat the disease.

❖ VITAMINS: ISOLATING SUBSTANCES ESSENTIAL TO HEALTH

Before the decade began, Dutch physician and pathologist Christiaan Eijkman (1858–1930) and British biochemist Frederick Hopkins (1861–1947) discovered that important nutrients are required to maintain good health. These nutrients became known as vitamins. For their discovery, Eijkman and Hopkins shared the Nobel Prize for physiology or medicine in 1929. Meanwhile, many researchers studied vitamins during the 1920s, and several new vitamins were discovered during the decade.

In 1922, Elmer McCollum (1879–1967) reported the discovery of vitamin D, a fat-soluble vitamin found in milk, egg yolks, and fish-liver oils. McCollum's research proved that vitamin D and sunlight were useful in combating rickets, a disease caused by a calcium deficiency that results in insufficient skeletal growth and deformed bones in children. Harry Steenbock (1886–1967) furthered McCollum's work by determining that exposure to sunlight converted chemicals found in food into vitamin D. Also in 1922, Herbert McLean Evans (1882–1971) and Katharine Scott Bishop (1889–1975) announced the discovery of vitamin E, a fat-soluble vitamin whose deficiency results in muscle and vascular abnormalities and infertility. In 1926, B.C.P. Jansen (1884–?) and W. F. Donath reported the isolation of vitamin B^1 (thiamine), utilized by the body to convert amino acids, fats, and carbohydrates into energy. In 1928, Albert Szent-Gyorgyi (1893–1986) reported the isolation of vitamin C (ascorbic acid), a water-soluble vitamin found in leafy vegetables and fruits. This discovery resulted in the eradication of scurvy, a disease whose symptoms included skin

Albert Szent-Gyorgyi earned the Nobel Prize in physiology or medicine in 1937 for isolating vitamin C. This discovery resulted in the eradication of scurvy. **Reproduced courtesy of the Library of Congress.**

discoloration, anemia, and tooth loss. Because no fresh fruits and vegetables were available on long sea voyages, scurvy was common among sailors. Finally, in 1929, Carl Dam (1895–1976) reported the discovery of vitamin K, a fat-soluble vitamin necessary for the clotting of blood.

Szent-Gyorgyi, a Hungarian-born chemist and biologist, earned the Nobel Prize in physiology or medicine in 1937 for isolating vitamin C. He accomplished this feat while experimenting on cell respiration, during which he separated a chemical from lemon- and orange-producing plants. He named this substance ascorbic acid, or vitamin C. Referring to the process by which researchers employ trial and error to achieve medical breakthroughs, Szent-Gyorgyi is credited with two significant observations: "A discovery is said to be an accident meeting a prepared mind"; and "Discovery is seeing what everybody else has seen and thinking what nobody else has thought."

 For More Information

BOOKS

Bachrach, Deborah. *The Importance of Margaret Sanger.* San Diego: Lucent Books, 1993.

Cefrey, Holly. *Syphilis and Other Sexually Transmitted Diseases.* New York: Rosen Publishing Group, 2002.

Denzel, Justin F. *Genius With a Scalpel: Harvey Cushing.* New York: Messner, 1971.

Ferber, Elizabeth. *Diabetes.* Brookfield, CT: Millbrook Press, 1996.

Hyde, Margaret O. *Know About Tuberculosis.* New York: Walker & Company, 1994.

Hyde, Margaret O., and Elizabeth H. Forsyth, MD. *Vaccinations: From Smallpox to Cancer.* New York: Franklin Watts, 2000.

Jacobs, Francine. *Breakthrough, the True Story of Penicillin.* New York: Dodd, Mead, 1985.

Landau, Elaine. *Diabetes.* New York: Twenty-First Century Books, 1994.

Landau, Elaine. *Tuberculosis.* New York: Franklin Watts, 1995.

Nardo, Don. *Vitamins and Minerals.* New York: Chelsea House, 1994.

Otfinoski, Steven. *Alexander Fleming: Conquering Disease with Penicillin.* New York: Facts on File, 1992.

Peacock, Judith. *Diabetes.* Mankato, MN: LifeMatters Press, 2000.

Silverstein, Alvin, Virginia Silverstein, and Robert Silverstein. *Measles and Rubella.* Springfield, NJ: Enslow Publishers, 1997.

Silverstein, Alvin, Virginia Silverstein, and Robert Silverstein. *Tuberculosis.* Hillside, NJ: Enslow Publishers, 1994.

Stewart, Gail. *Diabetes.* San Diego: Lucent Books, 1999.

Tocci, Salvatore. *Alexander Fleming: The Man Who Discovered Penicillin.* Berkeley Heights, NJ: Enslow Publishers, 2002.

Topalian, Elyse. *Margaret Sanger.* New York: Franklin Watts, 1984.

Whitelaw, Nancy. *Margaret Sanger: Every Child a Wanted Child.* New York: Dillon Press, 1994.

Yancey, Diane. *Tuberculosis.* Brookfield, CT: Twenty-First Century Books, 2001.

WEB SITES

Achievements in Public Health, 1900–1999: Healthier Mothers and Babies. http://www.cdc.gov/epo/mmwr/preview/mmwrhtml/mm4838a2.htm (accessed on August 5, 2002).

The Leaded Gas Scare of the 1920s. http://www.nrdc.org/air/transportation/hleadgas.asp (accessed on August 5, 2002).

Medicine and Madison Avenue—Timeline. http://scriptorium.lib.duke.edu/mma/timeline.html#1920 (accessed on August 2, 2002).

1920s. http://www.usgennet.org/usa/il/state/alhn1920.html (accessed on August 5, 2002).

Sanger Fact Sheet. http://www.plannedparenthood.org/about/thisispp/sanger.html (accessed on August 5, 2002).

chapter seven *Science and Technology*

1920: Ex-U.S. Army officer John Thompson patents his machine gun, later nicknamed the "tommy gun."

1920: October 27 The U.S. Department of Commerce issues a license to KDKA, the first commercial radio station in America.

1921: Thomas Midgley Jr. invents an improved gasoline by adding tetraethyl lead. It is marketed as Ethyl gasoline.

1921: August 23 The British R38 dirigible breaks in half, resulting in the deaths of forty-eight passengers. It is the worst aviation disaster to date.

1922: A team of scientists at Johns Hopkins University discovers vitamin D in cod liver oil.

1922: William Howell discovers heparin, which will be used as an anticoagulant (a substance that prevents the clotting of blood) in blood transfusions.

1922: February 27 U.S. Secretary of Commerce Herbert Hoover convenes a national conference of radio, telephone, and telegraph experts.

1922: December *The Toll of the Sea,* the first feature-length Technicolor motion picture, is released.

1923: Electrical engineer Edwin H. Armstrong constructs the first FM radio.

1923: Two U.S. Army pilots perform the first in-air refueling operation.

1923: Inventor and manufacturer George Eastman produces 16mm film for use by the general public, beginning the era of home movies.

1924: Transatlantic radio transmission of still photographs begins.

1924: American Telephone and Telegraph and General Electric unite their research divisions to form Bell Telephone Laboratories (also known as Bell Labs).

1925: Electrical engineer Vladimir Zworykin applies for a patent for color television.

1925: Pathologist George H. Whipple demonstrates that iron is an essential element in red blood cells.

1925: A microfilm camera is patented. It is used by banks to produce miniature copies of checks.

1926: The National Broadcasting Company (NBC) forms a "network" by linking twenty-four radio stations.

1926: The introduction of the mule-drawn cotton stripper marks the end of the labor-intensive practice of picking cotton by hand.

1926: A voiceprint machine, or voice coder, is developed by Bell Labs which can analyze the frequency (pitch) and energy content of speech.

1926: Chemist James B. Sumner demonstrates that enzymes are proteins and that they assist biochemical reactions in the body.

1926: Vitamin B¹ is discovered.

1926: **February 18** *Microbe Hunters,* by Paul de Kruif, is published and becomes one of the most popular books on bacteriology ever written.

1926: **March 16** Scientist Robert H. Goddard launches the first rocket propelled by liquid fuel.

1926: **August 6** *Don Juan,* the first feature-length motion picture with synchronized music and sound effects, premieres.

1927: J. A. O'Neill invents the first magnetic recording tape.

1927: **February 23** The U.S. Congress creates the Federal Radio Commission.

1927: **April 7** American Telephone & Telegraph (AT&T) sponsors the first successful demonstration of television,

in the Washington, D.C. office of Secretary of Commerce Herbert Hoover.

1927: **May 20–21** Charles A. Lindbergh makes the first solo flight across the Atlantic Ocean.

1927: **October** *The Jazz Singer,* the first feature-length motion picture with sequences that include singing and dialogue, premieres.

1927: **December** Henry Ford introduces the Model A automobile.

1928: Respiratory specialists Philip Drinker and Louis Shaw invent the "iron lung" as an aid to breathing.

1928: Minnesota Mining and Manufacturing (3M) Company markets cellophane tape as Scotch tape.

1928: Richard E. Byrd establishes a base in Antarctica from which he flies over the South Pole.

1928: Vitamin C is discovered.

1928: General Electric and New York radio station WRNY make the first primitive efforts at television broadcasting.

1929: The Dunlop Rubber Company develops the first foam rubber.

1929: **July 17** Robert Goddard launches the first instrumented rocket, complete with camera, barometer, and thermometer.

Overview

During the 1920s, ideas and inventions on which scientists and engineers had been working for years came out of the developmental stage and entered people's lives for the first time. For instance, the automobile became a fixture of everyday American life. The Ford Motor Company's classic Model T remained the most popular and affordable car. When sales began to slip, Henry Ford marketed a totally new design called the Model A. Meanwhile Chevrolet, a rival manufacturer, began encroaching on Ford's domination of the automobile industry.

The airplane had been in existence since the first years of the century, but it had not yet grown into a commercial industry. Former World War I (1914–18) pilots, unable to find postwar employment, purchased war planes and barnstormed across the nation, performing daredevil feats at country fairs. At the time, the skies were just as likely to hold a dirigible (a balloon-powered airship) as an airplane. As the decade progressed, however, airplanes increasingly were used to deliver mail across America. Day-and-night flying became commonplace. By decade's end, the major American cities were connected by regularly scheduled commercial air flights. On the military front, William "Billy" Mitchell, a U.S. Army Air Corps officer, became a vocal and controversial advocate for the establishment of an air force as an independent branch of the American military.

Since the late nineteenth century, attempts had been made to add sound to motion pictures, but problems of amplification and synchronization prevented these experimental systems from succeeding. From 1922 through 1925, Lee De Forest, Theodore Case, and E. I. Sponable devised a means for adding synchronized sound to film. Engineers at Western Electric and the Bell Laboratories also developed a sound-on-disc system for motion pictures. This system was employed by the Warner Bros. film studio in 1926 and 1927, when it began producing and releasing the first motion pictures featuring synchronized music, sound effects, and dialogue. Their immediate popularity spelled doom for silent films and revolutionized the industry. During the decade, a number of motion pictures also were filmed using the Technicolor process. American entertainment underwent further upheaval with the growth of radio. The first commercial radio station came into being at the decade's start. Others followed, and the new medium eventually became a multimillion-dollar business.

The 1920s saw the invention and marketing of a range of new (or improved) products and processes. Magnetic tape, cellophane tape, and foam rubber were developed during the decade. So were the polygraph (lie detector) and the iron lung. Several vitamins were discovered or identified. Scientists explored the heavens and conducted experiments involving the nature and composition of matter. The first successful helicopter flight was completed during the decade. So was the initial solo, nonstop transatlantic flight, which proved to be the decade's most heralded technical feat. In 1927, Charles A. Lindbergh, a young aviator, departed Long Island, New York, in his small custom-built plane, "The Spirit of St. Louis." Thirty-three-and-a-half hours later, he landed in France. Lindbergh promptly became one of the decade's heroes.

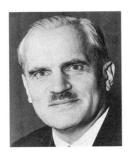

Arthur Holly Compton (1892–1962) While researching the nature of matter during the early 1920s, physicist Arthur Holly Compton discovered what came to be known as the Compton effect: When an X ray strikes an electron, it bounces off at an angle to its original trajectory and loses energy in the process. He published his findings in 1923 and was awarded a share of the 1927 Nobel Prize in physics. The following year, Compton coined the word *photon* (a significant packet of radiant energy or light). During World War II, he worked on the Manhattan project to develop the atomic bomb. *Photo reproduced by permission of Archive Photos, Inc.*

Edwin P. Hubble (1889–1953) In 1923, Edwin P. Hubble aimed the powerful 100-inch telescope located at the Mount Wilson Observatory in Pasadena, California, in the direction of the Andromeda nebulae. He believed Andromeda was not merely a gas cloud or a fuzzy single star but rather a collection of stars that were a million light years away from Earth. Building on the work of Vesto Slipher (1875–1969), Hubble next began to examine the different galaxies. His calculations that they constantly are moving away from each other paved the way for the Big Bang theory, the most widely accepted scientific explanation for the origin of the universe.

Photo reproduced by permission of the Corbis Corporation.

Charles A. Lindbergh (1902–1974) On May 20 and 21, 1927, Charles A. Lindbergh stunned the world by flying solo from New York to Paris. His accomplishment won him instant celebrity, and deeply affected the development of aviation. It proved the possibility of building safe planes capable of flying long distances, and led to the creation of commercial airlines and specialized military aircraft. Lindbergh eventually became a tragic and controversial figure. The kidnapping and murder of his infant son in 1932 shocked the nation, and the crime resulted in passage of a federal kidnapping law (commonly known as the Lindbergh Act). He was soundly criticized by many of his fellow Americans for the pro-German isolationist stance he took before World War II (1939–45). *Photo reproduced by permission of the Corbis Corporation.*

Margaret Mead (1901–1978) Margaret Mead was perhaps the twentieth century's foremost cultural anthropologist. Between November 1925 and June 1926, she lived in the Samoan Islands, where she studied the native language and interviewed about fifty Samoan adolescent females. Upon noting the differences between them and their American counterparts, she concluded that culture, rather than biology, has the greater impact on individual personality. Mead published her findings in her classic study, *Coming of Age in Samoa* (1928), which was hailed as a breakthrough with regard to the importance of nurturing, or upbringing, in individual development. It became a best-seller. *Photo reproduced by permission of Archive Photos, Inc.*

Albert A. Michelson (1852–1931) Albert A. Michelson, a longtime professor at the University of Chicago, spent his summers at the California Institute of Technology and the nearby Mount Wilson Observatory. Using the 100-inch telescope at the observatory, he attempted to measure the diameter of a star. He selected Betelgeuse (pronounced BEETLE-juice), the largest star in the constellation Orion, and he employed trigonometry to calculate its diameter as 386 million kilometers (240 million miles). In December 1920, it was announced that Michelson was the first to measure the size of a star other than the Sun. *Photo reproduced courtesy of the Library of Congress.*

Robert A. Millikan (1868–1953) In 1923, Robert A. Millikan won the Nobel Prize in physics for charting the course of water and oil droplets flying through the air. It was a study he had undertaken in an attempt to find the absolute charge of the electron, and he had completed this work in 1917. Millikan spent the 1920s exploring the nature and origin of radioactivity. In mid-decade, he proved that radioactivity originated in outer space, rather than on Earth. He dubbed these emissions *cosmic rays* and continued to investigate this mysterious energy. *Photo reproduced courtesy of the Library of Congress.*

Igor Sikorsky (1889–1972) Russian emigré Igor Sikorsky was one of the decade's great American aircraft designers. In 1913, Sikorsky built and flew the first multimotored airplane. In 1920, he formed a partnership to manufacture large airplanes capable of carrying freight or passengers. Three years later, the company became the Sikorsky Aero Engineering Company. Sikorsky successfully tested the two-engine, fourteen-passenger S-29-A. Then he began building the S-37, which he sold to American Airways International. In 1929, the S-37 flew 7,000 miles, from San Francisco to Santiago, Chile. Other Sikorsky innovations included a twin-engine amphibian plane and the first operable helicopters. *Photo reproduced courtesy of the Library of Congress.*

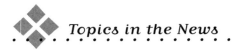

Topics in the News . . . .

❖ AUTOMOBILES: FORD AND CHEVROLET LEAD THE COMPETITION

During the 1920s, the story of the motorcar remained the story of Henry Ford (1863–1947). This giant of American industry continued to dominate the field of automotive production and engineering. Between 1908 and 1926, more than fifteen million of his Model T's, the Ford Motor Company's mass-produced automobile model, were sold. Then in 1927, Ford introduced his new Model A. This was no retooled, restyled Model T; rather, it was a completely new automobile with a safety-glass windshield, hydraulic shock absorbers, an all-wheel braking system, and a high-geared transmission.

The Ford Motor Company did not monopolize the American automobile industry, however. Chevrolet also kept adding new styles of cars, each with improved engineering. In 1927, the year Ford shifted models, Chevrolet actually outsold Ford for the first time by marketing over one million vehicles. The following year, with the Model A in full production, Ford regained the sales lead only to lose it again in 1929. That year, Chevrolet added a bold innovation: the "valve-in-head" engine design (in which the valve compartments are parts of a single, precast engine block). This design would become the standard in the automotive industry.

Across the decades, the Ford Motor Company remained one of America's leading automobile producers. Yet it never again thoroughly dominated the industry as it had during the first quarter of the twentieth century.

❖ AVIATION: PILOTS SEEK PEACETIME EMPLOYMENT

During World War I (1914–18), military aircraft technology went through exceptional (not to mention rapid) development. In the decade that followed, civilian pursuits dominated the aviation world.

Ex-fighter pilots, who had battled their nation's enemies during the war, now were unemployed. The commercial airline industry was in its infancy, and there were no jobs awaiting them. So for a few hundred dollars, many pilots purchased war-surplus planes, usually two-seater Curtiss JN-4 "Jenny" trainers, and barnstormed (toured rural areas to perform shows). They flew from county fair to county fair, offering rides to one person at a time for the then-significant fee of $5 or $10. These romantic daredevils became the subjects of movies, in which they were shown flying upside down, under bridges, and through barns. In fact, one of the

"Boss Kett" was the beloved nickname of Charles Franklin Kettering (1876–1958), the man responsible for some of the most important innovations in the automobile industry. By 1920, he already was acclaimed as the inventor of the electric self-starter: a motor that turned over the engine of the car, eliminating the necessity of dangerous and laborious hand-cranking. During the decade, Kettering was vice president for research at General Motors (GM). He worked on the development of leaded gasoline, which increased octane and prevented engine knock. He helped to develop Duco, a durable, fast-drying lacquer finish for auto bodies. When Duco was introduced in 1925, it came in only one color: light blue. GM chemists eventually came up with additional colors.

Perhaps Kettering's greatest accomplishment during the decade was the development of a high-speed, two-cycle diesel engine (an internal combustion engine in which fuel is ignited when air is compressed until it reaches a high temperature). During the following decade, this engine revolutionized the manner in which the world powered its trucks, ships, and locomotives.

decade's hit movies, and the first film to win a Best Picture Academy Award, was titled *Wings* (1927). Its characters, however, were not stunt flyers, but all-American boys fighting in World War I. The film featured combat flying sequences that dazzled audiences.

In the 1920s, anyone able to operate an airplane could fly one. There were no official inspections of aircraft, no mandatory pilot training, and no rules of flight. In 1926, the U.S. Congress passed an Air Commerce Act, creating an Aeronautics Branch connected to the Department of Commerce. Planes and pilots became subject to qualification standards and licensing, and the recklessness of the barnstormers came to an end. As the decade progressed, the best way for a pilot to make steady money in aviation was by taking a job with a private company or landing a government contract to deliver mail.

The first regular airmail route had been established in 1918 between New York and Washington, D.C. Two years later, the U.S. Post Office expanded its airmail service across the continent, initiating a route between New York and San Francisco with stops in major cities. Initially, mail was airborne only during the day and was transported by train at night. Day-and-night air transportation was attempted in 1921, but discontinued because of the dangers of night flying. In fact, flying after dark was the main cause for the deadly crashes of thirty-one of the first forty airmail planes. Not until mid–1924 was day-and-night airmail service permanently established. Meanwhile, passenger service on airplanes was slower to develop. Flying was uncomfortable, and most people feared potential air accidents. Despite this, the end of the decade saw the major American cities linked by regularly scheduled airline service.

While the decade was not an active period for the evolution of military aircraft, the armed services remained involved in aviation. U.S. Army Air Corps Brig. Gen. William "Billy" Mitchell (1879–1936) was the champion of military aviation. Mitchell steered U.S. aviation during World War I (1914–18), and in the 1920s he became a vocal, controversial advocate of the establishment of an air force: a military branch to be operated inde-

Charles Lindbergh loading a sack of mail. As the 1920s progressed, many pilots were able to earn steady money by landing government contracts for delivering mail. Reproduced by permission of the Corbis Corporation.

pendently of the U.S. Army and Navy. In 1921, Mitchell demonstrated the potential of air power by showing how airplanes could be used to help sink large naval vessels. Yet several of his superiors questioned his testing procedures. Upon harassing his critics, he was demoted. In 1925, Mitchell was court-martialed for insubordination after blaming the crash of the dirigible (a balloon-powered airship with a rigid hull structure) *Shenandoah* on "incompetency and criminal neglect." After being suspended from active duty for five years, he resigned, and his downfall hurt efforts to win congressional appropriations for military aviation in the late 1920s. (During this time, private aeronautics were assisted financially by the Guggenheim Fund for the Promotion of Aeronautics, a philanthropic fund established by American mining entrepreneur Daniel Guggenheim [1856–1930].) It was not until World War II (1939–45) that Mitchell's dream of an independent U.S. Air Force was realized.

During the decade, airplanes were used as racers. From 1920 to 1925, army and navy planes and civilian sports planes were entered in the National Air Races and other international meets. The competing planes, primarily built for speed, included a range of single- and double-seat models with high-compression engines. In 1925, U.S. Army Lieutenant James H. "Jimmy" Doolittle (1896–1993) set a world air speed record of 245.7 miles per hour while competing in the Schneider Trophy Race. Doolittle was enlisted by the Guggenheim Fund to perform aeronautical experiments that led to the development of instrument flying, which minimized crashes caused by fog or night blindness. The fund also assisted American aviator and explorer Richard E. Byrd (1888–1957) on his polar expeditions.

In 1925, Byrd headed up the air unit that accompanied an Arctic expedition led by Donald B. MacMillan (1874–1970). This group was sponsored by the National Geographic Society. Its purpose was to experiment with the use of airplanes and shortwave radio in the Arctic. That same year, Byrd flew over the North Pole. Three years later, he flew over the South Pole. Starting in 1928, he made the first of five major expeditions to Antarctica.

❖ AVIATION: "LUCKY LINDY" CROSSES THE ATLANTIC

Pioneer aviator Charles A. Lindbergh (1902–1974) was one of the most celebrated Americans of the 1920s. He earned his fame for accomplishing the decade's greatest and most publicized aeronautic feat: a solo, nonstop crossing of the Atlantic Ocean, which Lindbergh accomplished in 1927.

Lindbergh's flight was not the first Atlantic air crossing. Eight years earlier, five Navy fliers piloted a seaplane, the NC-4, from Newfoundland, Canada to the Azores to Portugal and finally to England. Still, no one ever had flown solo from America to Europe. Lindbergh was determined to do so. He was backed by civic boosters and aviation buffs from St. Louis, Missouri; for this reason, he named his plane "The Spirit of St. Louis." The plane was specially constructed for the flight. It featured a nine-cylinder, air-cooled Curtiss-Wright engine with redundancies (back-up parts), such as two ignition systems and a double carburetor. Lindbergh supervised and assisted in the plane's construction, which was accomplished in sixty days at a cost of $10,580.

On May 10, 1927, Lindbergh left San Diego (where "The Spirit of St. Louis" had been built) for New York, making a brief stop in St. Louis. On May 12, he landed at Roosevelt Field on Long Island. After a week of final preparations, interviews, and weather-watching, the U.S. Weather Bureau issued a guardedly optimistic forecast for the North Atlantic. The date was May 20. It was pouring rain at Roosevelt Field, but Lindbergh optimistically ordered his plane pushed out of its hangar and into take-off position. The flier and his plane bumped across the muddy airstrip, barely reaching sufficient speed to clear a parked tractor and some overhead wires at the end of the runway. Finally, at 7:52 A.M., Lindbergh was completely airborne. "The Spirit of St. Louis" carried 425 gallons of gasoline. Its cockpit was completely stripped down. It contained no radio and no parachute. To minimize the plane's weight, its cockpit seat was made of wicker (interlaced twigs), rather than metal. The only food Lindbergh carried on board was five sandwiches.

As he flew, Lindbergh was aware that his greatest enemy was lack of sleep. He had prepared for the flight by deliberately depriving himself of sleep for long periods. Before reaching Nova Scotia, he fell asleep, then woke up with a jolt. Upon opening a window to allow cold air to blow onto his face, the chart on which he had plotted his course almost was sucked out of the plane. Lindbergh buzzed (flew low) the "Spirit" over St. John's, Newfoundland, to signal his presence. Then he headed out over the vastness of the open Atlantic. By then, he was flying blindly in dense clouds. In an effort to rise above them, he attempted to increase his altitude to over ten thousand feet. As he climbed, the plane's wings began to ice up. Lindbergh quickly descended, thereby escaping the ice and clouds.

Just as he had figured, sleeplessness continued to strain him. He hallucinated. He dozed off. Sometimes, he snapped awake just as the "Spirit" was about to set down in the Atlantic. Eventually, Lindbergh observed the Irish coast. He fixed his position and headed for his final destination: Paris. A tumultuous crowd of one hundred thousand excited French men and women awaited his arrival at Le Bourget airport. A cheering throng surged onto the runway as Lindbergh taxied to a stop. His epic flight of 3,610 miles took him thirty-three-and-a-half hours. Lindbergh did not fly the "Spirit" back to the United States. Instead, he returned home on board the U.S. Navy cruiser *Memphis*. The media dubbed him "Lucky Lindy" and the "Lone Eagle." He was presented awards and made the subject of popular songs. President Calvin Coolidge (1872–1933) bestowed on Lindbergh the Congressional Medal of Honor and the Distinguished Flying Cross.

❖ DIRIGIBLES: FLOATING ACROSS THE SKY

During the 1920s, airplanes were not the only aircraft that took to the skies. Such lighter-than-air craft as dirigibles and blimps (nonrigid airships with limp hull structures that fell flat when deflated) swept across the skies. These airships were devised in France during the late eighteenth century. They remained strictly experimental for more than a century, until Count Ferdinand von Zeppelin (1838–1917), a German aeronautical engineer, designed and constructed fewer than one hundred powered balloons, which were named for him. Zeppelins were employed by the Germans on bombing raids over England during World War I (1914–18). The huge crafts soaked up antiaircraft fire before floating back behind German lines.

A U.S. Navy blimp. Although devised in France in the late eighteenth century, blimps remained strictly experimental for more than a century. **Reproduced by permission of the Corbis Corporation.**

In 1920, the U.S. Navy contracted with the British government to purchase their R38 dirigible. A crew was sent abroad to be trained to operate the ship and fly it back to America. Tragically, the airship broke in half during a strenuous test run over Hull, England, in 1921. Like the German airships, the R38 was filled with highly flammable hydrogen. The breakage started fires on board, and forty-four passengers, sixteen of whom were American, were killed. It was the worst aviation disaster in history up to that time.

In 1923 the *Shenandoah*, the initial American-made dirigible, went airborne. Unlike its predecessors, the *Shenandoah* was the first rigid airship to be filled with helium. Helium is not flammable like hydrogen, but it also weighs more and thus has less lifting ability. Helium also was extremely expensive; in the 1920s, it cost over two hundred times more than hydrogen. In 1924, the *Shenandoah* was joined in its home hangar in Lakehurst, New Jersey, by the *Los Angeles,* its German-made sister ship. There was insignificant helium available to lift both dirigibles, which kept the *Shenandoah* out of commission until June 1925. That September, it left Lakehurst to commence its fifty-seventh flight, a public-relations tour of large cities and state fairs in the Midwest. While floating near Ava, Ohio, the ship encountered a fierce line of thunderstorms. It rose uncontrollably, with violent rolling and pitching. Then it dived out of control. Within three minutes, the *Shenandoah* dropped more than three thousand feet. The crew discharged ballast (a weighty substance employed to control the dirigible's ascent), and the ship leveled out. But two minutes later, it was caught in another updraft. This time, the *Shenandoah* broke in half, spilling out some of its crew. Eventually, the survivors managed to maneuver the forward part of the ship to a relatively soft landing. Fourteen members of the forty-three person crew died, including the ship's captain.

Meanwhile, the *Los Angeles* remained in active service for eight years, a lengthy time for a dirigible. It completed 331 flights and was retired in 1932.

❖ HELICOPTERS: A NEW FLYING MACHINE

In 1922 Emile Berliner (1851–1929), who previously had invented the microphone, and his son Henry made the first successful helicopter flight. While the helicopter attained an altitude of only fifteen to twenty feet and flew at just twenty miles per hour, the flight was significant because the machine rose from the ground and then flew horizontally. At the time, other experimental aircraft could rise and set down vertically but were incapable of horizontal movement.

In 1909 and 1910, before he emigrated to the United States from Russia, aeronautical engineer and aircraft designer Igor Sikorsky (1889–1972) had constructed two prototype helicopters. Neither would fly, however. Sikorsky decided that his work on the helicopter would have to wait for "better engines, lighter materials, and experienced mechanics." In the 1930s, he returned to work on rotary-bladed aircraft and developed the first truly workable helicopters.

❖ THE LIE DETECTOR: A NEW INVESTIGATIVE TOOL

In the early 1920s, John Augustus Larson (1892–1983), a Berkeley, California police officer, developed the first practical polygraph. With three pens swinging back and forth on a slowly moving strip of paper, Larson's polygraph measured changes in his subject's blood pressure, heart rate, and breathing rate. Leonarde Keeler (c. 1904–1949), who worked with Larson, added a fourth measurement: changes in perspiration. Because these indicators allegedly would increase when a subject lied, the moving pens were supposed to swing more widely when untruths were spoken.

As the lie detector evolved, a trained operator asked the subject a series of "control" questions. This established a base pattern of readings against which to compare deviations. Early operators also mixed relevant and irrelevant questions, a tactic that Larson himself faulted. This tactic was abandoned in large part by the 1950s.

Larson and Keeler never stated that their machine could measure a subject's candor with 100 percent accuracy. Indeed, skeptics then and now have claimed that some people under examination might be so nervous and intimidated that their sessions would produce plenty of false readings. Even though polygraph machines and operators have become more sophisticated across the decades, reservations about their reliability remain, and lie detector results continue to be inadmissible as evidence in most courts of law.

❖ MOVIES WITH SOUND: SILENCE NO LONGER IS GOLDEN

The 1920s were the golden age of the silent motion picture. American movie fans by the millions flocked to see comedies, dramas, and action-adventure films that were acted without words. While the movie played, pianists often accompanied the action on the screen with appropriate background music to enhance the mood. In the larger theaters, located in major cities, full orchestras even played live music for their patrons.

Since the dawn of the motion picture in the 1890s, inventors and visionaries had attempted to unite sight and sound on screen. The problem stymied Thomas Alva Edison (1847–1931), perhaps the greatest inventor in American history. In 1895 and 1913, he produced devices to accomplish this goal, called Kinetophones, that were failures. Attempts by others, resulting in such contraptions as the Synchroscope, the Cinematophone, and the Cameraphone, also misfired. Some, however, were promising. From 1922 through 1925, Lee De Forest, Theodore Case, and E. I. Sponable devised a system for photographing synchronized sound on film, which was called Phonofilm. In 1960, the Motion Picture Academy of Arts and Sciences (MPAA) awarded De Forest a special Academy Award "for his pioneering inventions which brought sound to the motion picture."

In the 1920s, radio engineers at Western Electric and telephone engineers at Bell Laboratories worked on a sound system for films. Sam Warner (1887–1927), one of the four brothers who founded the then-struggling Warner Bros. studio, learned of their efforts. Warner believed that talking pictures which actually worked might be a bonanza for his company. He mentioned this to his brother Harry (1881–1958), who allegedly responded, "Who the hell wants to hear actors talk?" Nonetheless, Harry became convinced of the potential for talking pictures. In 1926, Warner Bros. established a subsidiary company, Vitaphone, in conjunction with Western Electric. Their goal was to implement a sound-on-disc system for motion pictures. In this process, large phonograph records were played on a special projector-turntable system. The sounds emanating from the disc were synchronized to the onscreen images.

Vitaphone first produced and released several experimental short films. Before the year was out, it released *Don Juan,* a feature-length swashbuckler. While its actors did not speak, *Don Juan* featured synchronized music (recorded by the New York Philharmonic) and sound effects. Then in the summer of 1927, the studio produced *The Jazz Singer,* a melodrama with musical numbers starring Al Jolson (1886–1950), a popular stage entertainer. While essentially a silent film, *The Jazz Singer* did feature a synchronized soundtrack that included background music and sound effects. One sequence featured dialogue; Jolson prophetically blurted out the lines "Wait a minute. Wait a minute. You ain't heard nothing yet." The film's phenomenal box office success marked the beginning of the end for silent film. Sadly, Sam Warner died the evening before the film's New York premiere.

Warner Bros. then released its first all-talking picture, *Lights of New York* (1928). Other studios quickly began producing sound films, which became known as "talkies." Walt Disney (1901–1966) completed his first animated talkie, *Steamboat Willie,* in 1928, starring Mickey Mouse. Fox Studios released its first sound Western, *In Old Arizona,* in 1929; *Variety,* the show business trade magazine, described it as "the first outdoor talker" and noted, "…that it's right for box office is unquestioned at this time." Legendary film-

In the 1920s, important research was being carried out in computer and television technology. Even so, it would be decades before the fruits of this research affected American life.

During the decade, American electrical engineer Vannevar Bush (1890–1974) and a team of Massachusetts Institute of Technology (MIT) scientists began work on devising a "differential analyzer": the world's first analog computer (which was operated by numbers derived from such measurable quantities as rotations or voltages). In 1923 and 1924, Russian-born American electrical engineer Vladimir Zworykin (1889–1982) applied for a patent for his kinescope, an electronic scanning device for recording television programming.

maker Alfred Hitchcock (1899–1980) directed the first British-made, feature-length talkie, *Blackmail,* in 1929. The advent of the sound film also saw the birth of a new motion picture genre: the movie musical.

The success of these "all-talking, all-singing, all-dancing" motion pictures resulted in a major upheaval in the motion picture industry. Previously, screen actors were selected for their ability to physically act out roles. Speaking voices were unimportant, because they were unnecessary to an actor's performance. Now, Hollywood stars with thick foreign accents or thin, tinny voices found themselves unemployable. Meanwhile, the motion picture studios began importing actors from the Broadway stage: performers whose voices were trained. Hollywood movie sets had to be equipped with sound-recording equipment, and theaters needed to be furnished with sound systems.

❖ MOVIES IN COLOR: ADDING BRIGHTNESS TO MOTION PICTURE SCREENS

The employment of color film stock in motion pictures was pioneered by Herbert T. Kalmus (1881–1963), an educator who had studied at the Massachusetts Institute of Technology (MIT) and the University of Zurich. In 1912, he established the Technicolor Company and began experimenting with color film processes. In 1917, Kalmus produced a short color film, *The Gulf Between,* in which he superimposed two strips of film with different primary colors. Despite its novelty, *The Gulf Between* received little notice.

During the early 1920s, Kalmus made significant improvements over his original technique. He developed a process whereby two layers of film were exposed, dyed (one in red-orange, the other in blue-green), and photographically printed onto one another in a film laboratory. This process first was employed during the filming of *The Toll of the Sea* (1922). Other two-strip Technicolor shorts and feature-length films were produced during the decade, most notably *The Black Pirate* (1926), a swashbuckler. Kalmus eventually developed a three-strip process. *La Cucaracha* (1933) and *Becky Sharp* (1935) would be the first short and feature-length films shot using the three-strip process.

❖ THE RADIO BOOM: COMMERCIAL RADIO IN ITS INFANCY

Back in 1901, Italian physicist and inventor Guglielmo Marconi (1874–1937), one of the pioneers in the evolution of radio, had successfully received the first transatlantic radio communication, transmitted from England to Canada. Yet by 1920, radio still was in its experimental stages. This was despite the U.S. government's taking control of the medium during World War I (1914–18) and funding research into wireless technology.

During the war, developments in vacuum tubes (devices similar to lightbulbs and the ancestors of the modern transistor) allowed the sending and receiving of radio signals to become far more precise and powerful. In 1918, Edwin H. Armstrong (1890–1954) developed the super-heterodyne radio receiver, which allowed for the reception of a wide range of radio transmissions. The following year, this receiver went into production. Such advances allowed for the advent of the commercial radio industry in the early 1920s: An industry that would revolutionize mass commu-

An early radio receiver. During the 1920s the radio industry would revolutionize mass communication, as well as the manner in which millions of people across the world were entertained and informed. Reproduced by permission of the Corbis Corporation.

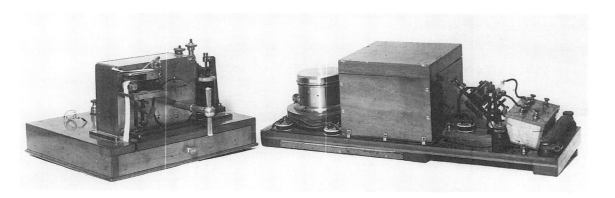

nication, as well as the manner in which millions of people across the world were entertained, enlightened, and pitched to by advertisers.

The first commercial radio station was started in east Pittsburgh, Pennsylvania by Frank Conrad (1874–1941), a Westinghouse engineer. Conrad, who was experimenting with voice-transmitting equipment for the U.S. Navy, set up a small radio in his garage. He tested his equipment by communicating with the Westinghouse plant some four or five miles away. In April 1920, Conrad received a license to use the call letters 8XK, and began communicating with a circle of radio-buff friends living in the Pittsburgh area. Additionally, he began playing phonograph records over the air. A local department store learned of Conrad's enterprise and placed an advertisement in the *Pittsburgh Sun,* hoping to sell radio receivers to those who might want to listen to Conrad's "programming." Conrad's work led Westinghouse to establish its own radio station, KDKA, which broadcast from a more powerful transmitter located on the roof of its Pittsburgh factory. In October 1920, the U.S. Department of Commerce licensed the station to operate at a wavelength of 360 meters. One of its most important early broadcasts reported the returns from the 1920 presidential election, in which Republican Warren G. Harding (1865–1923) ran against Democrat James M. Cox (1870–1957).

Due to pending litigation involving hundreds of radio-related patents, additional radio stations did not immediately flood the market. Nonetheless, commercial stations did begin to appear. A second station, WEAF in New York, began broadcasting in September 1921. By the end of 1922, there were 508 stations nationwide. In 1921, $9 million worth of radio equipment was sold. Two years later, that figure increased to $46 million. By 1926, it was up to $400 million. In 1922, sixty thousand radios could be found in American households. By 1933, there would be almost twenty million. The April 1923 issue of *Scientific American* magazine noted that "1922 will stand out in the history of radio. For it was during the past year that radio broadcasting became a regular feature of every-day life, and radio entered the average home life of the average man."

For More Information

BOOKS

Allen, Frederick Lewis. *Only Yesterday: An Informal History of the 1920s.* New York: Perennial Classics, 2000 (reprint edition).

Barr, Roger. *Radio: Wireless Sound.* San Diego: Lucent Books, 1994.

Datnow, Claire L. *Edwin Hubble: Discoverer of Galaxies.* Springfield, NJ: Enslow Publishers, 1997.

Denenberg, Barry. *An American Hero: The True Story of Charles A. Lindbergh*. New York: Scholastic, 1996.

Dolan, Terrance. *Probing Deep Space*. New York: Chelsea House, 1993.

Finkelstein, Norman H. *Sounds in the Air: The Golden Age of Radio*. New York: Atheneum, 1993.

Fox, Mary Virginia. *Edwin Hubble: American Astronomer*. New York: Franklin Watts, 1997.

Giblin, James. *Charles A. Lindbergh: A Human Hero*. New York: Clarion Books, 1997.

Grierson, John. *I Remember Lindbergh*. New York: Harcourt Brace, 1977.

Kent, Zachary. *Charles Lindbergh and the Spirit of St. Louis in American History*. Berkeley Heights, NJ: Enslow Publishers, 2001.

Mark, Joan. *Margaret Mead: Coming of Age in America*. New York: Oxford University Press, 1999.

Maurer, Richard. *Rocket! How a Toy Launched the Space Age*. New York: Crown Publishers, 1995.

McCarthy, Pat. *Henry Ford: Building Cars for Everyone*. Berkeley Heights, NJ: Enslow Publishers, 2002.

Meachum, Virginia. *Charles Lindbergh: American Hero of Flight*. Berkeley Heights, NJ: Enslow Publishers, 2002.

Pfleuger, Lynda. *George Eastman: Bringing Photography to the People*. Berkeley Heights, NJ: Enslow Publishers, 2002.

Pollard, Michael. *Margaret Mead: Bringing World Cultures Together*. Woodbridge, CT: Blackbirch Press, 1999.

Weitzman, David. *Model T: How Henry Ford Built a Legend*. New York: Crown Publishers, 2002.

Ziesk, Edra. *Margaret Mead: Anthropologist*. New York: Chelsea House, 1990.

WEB SITES

Media History Timeline: 1920s. http://www.mediahistory.umn.edu/time/1920s.html (accessed on August 5, 2002).

1920s. http://www.richland2.org/svh/Media/socstud/1920s.htm (accessed on August 5, 2002).

1920s. http://www.usgennet.org/usa/il/state/alhn1920.html (accessed on August 5, 2002).

The 1920s: Science, Nature, the Humanities. http://www.louisville.edu/~kprayb01/1920s-Science.html (accessed on August 2, 2002).

TIME Person of the Year Archive—Charles Lindbergh, 1927. http://www.time.com/time/poy2000/archive/1927.html (accessed on August 5, 2002).

chapter eight *Sports*

1920: **February 13** The Negro National League is organized in Kansas City, Missouri.

1920: **May 1** In major league baseball, Leon Cadore of Brooklyn and Joe Oeschger of Boston each pitch twenty-six innings in a 1 to 1 tie.

1920: **July 10** The racehorse Man o' War sets a world record by beating John P. Grier in a match race at Aqueduct.

1920: **August 16** Cleveland Indians shortstop Ray Chapman is hit in the head by New York Yankees' pitcher Carl Mays and dies the following day.

1920: **August 20** The formation of what would become the National Football League (NFL) is set in motion when representatives from several Ohio-based professional football teams meet in Canton, Ohio.

1920: **October 3** The St. Louis Browns' George Sisler sets a major league season record with his 257th hit.

1920: **October 10** Cleveland Indians second baseman Bill Wambsganss makes an unassisted triple play in the World Series.

1921: **January 12** Judge Kenesaw Mountain Landis is appointed major league baseball's first commissioner.

1921: **August 2** Eight members of the 1919 Chicago White Sox are acquitted on charges of fixing the World Series. However, Commissioner Landis bans them from baseball for life. The banned players become known as the "Black Sox."

1921: **November 25** The American Olympic Association is created; it is the permanent controlling board for American Olympic teams.

1922: **May** The U.S. Supreme Court decrees that baseball is not interstate commerce and thus is exempt from antitrust laws.

1922: **August 26** The U.S. defeats Great Britain and Ireland in the first Walker Cup golf matches.

1923: **April 18** Yankee Stadium opens in New York.

1923: **October 15** The New York Yankees win their first world championship.

1924: The Boston Bruins become the first U.S. team to join the National Hockey League (NHL).

1924: **January 25–February 4** The first Winter Olympic Games are held in Chamonix, France.

1924: **September 28** The Chicago Cardinals' Paddy Driscoll drop-kicks a 55-yard field goal in professional football.

1924: **October 5** The St. Louis Cardinals' Rogers Hornsby hits .424, the twentieth century's highest major league baseball batting average.

1924: **October 18** Illinois halfback Harold "Red" Grange scores four touchdowns in twelve minutes against the Michigan football team.

1925: **June 1** The Yankees' Lou Gehrig plays the first of his record 2,130 consecutive games.

1925: **November 26** A new Madison Square Garden stadium opens in New York.

1926: **February 16** Suzanne Lenglen defeats Helen Wills in the tennis "Match of the Century."

1926: **April** The New York Rangers, Chicago Blackhawks, and Detroit Cougars join the NHL.

1926: **August 6** Gertrude Ederle becomes the first woman to swim the English Channel.

1926: **September 23** Gene Tunney defeats Jack Dempsey to become the heavyweight boxing champion.

1927: **June 5** The U.S. defeats Great Britain in the first Ryder Cup golf competition.

1927: **September 30** Babe Ruth hits his sixtieth home run, breaking the record he set in 1921.

1928: **April 15** The New York Rangers become the first American hockey team to win the Stanley Cup championship.

1928: **September 3** Ty Cobb pinch-hits a double in a game against the Washington Senators. It is the last of his 4,189 major league hits.

1928: **December 11** National League President John Heydler suggests the use of a designated hitter for pitchers.

1929: **January 1** Roy Riegels runs 63 yards to the wrong goalpost and sets up a score for Georgia Tech, who beat Riegels' team, the University of California, Berkeley, 8 to 7 in the Rose Bowl game.

1929: **July 5** The New York Giants become the first baseball team to employ a public address system in a major league ballpark.

1929: **November 28** Ernie Nevers scores all forty points for the Chicago Cardinals in a 40 to 6 NFL victory over the Chicago Bears.

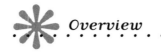

Overview

The 1920s is considered the golden age of American sports. The Great War (1914–18) in Europe had finally ended, and Americans were eager to forget the fighting and enjoy themselves. What's more, the economy was booming along with the stock market. It was a time for escapism, and fans rooted wildly for their favorite athletes and the teams for which they played. Three sports dominated the decade: professional baseball, college football, and boxing. Athletes, particularly those who starred in these sports, became national and international heroes and were revered by sports and nonsports fans alike. In some cases, the awe-inspiring feats they accomplished redefined their sports.

Babe Ruth, arguably the most famous athlete of the decade, had a greater impact on professional baseball than any single player in history. At the beginning of the 1920s, the sport was reeling from the Black Sox scandal. Eight Chicago White Sox players were alleged to have had knowledge of or actively conspired in a plot to throw (intentionally lose) the 1919 World Series. While all of the players were cleared of the charges in court, the integrity of the game had to be maintained, so the authorities banned them from baseball for life. Public confidence in the integrity of the game was low. But Ruth won over fans by belting bunches of home runs. The pre-Ruth period in baseball was known as the "dead-ball era." A ballplayer might hit a dozen or so home runs and lead the league in that category. In 1920, however, Ruth hit fifty-four home runs. The following season, he bashed fifty-nine. Then, in 1927, he smashed sixty.

During the decade, football primarily was a college game. Among individual players, Harold "Red" Grange of the University of Illinois and Ernie Nevers of Stanford were masters of the gridiron. Among teams,

Notre Dame dominated under legendary coach Knute Rockne. However, professional football took root at the beginning of the decade with the establishment of the American Professional Football Association (APFA), which quickly changed its name to the National Football League (NFL). While the league and the sport, at least on a professional level, did not come to rival baseball as a national pastime until the 1950s, the NFL did survive the decade.

The 1920s was a special era for boxing, with such ring legends as Jack Dempsey, Gene Tunney, and Benny Leonard, making headlines. The second Dempsey-Tunney title fight was perhaps the 1920s greatest fight because of its celebrated and controversial "long count," where Dempsey stood over Tunney after flooring him. This added four extra seconds to the normal ten-second count and saved Tunney from defeat. The decade saw the sport become a glamour profession, with over one hundred thousand fans pouring into arenas for title bouts and gate revenues topping $1 million.

Other master athletes reigned during the decade. Among them were golfers Bobby Jones, Walter Hagen, and Gene Sarazen, Many consider Jones the greatest golfer, not just of the decade, but of the twentieth century. Bill Tilden, became the first tennis star to win national celebrity. Women athletes also earned acclaim. Among them were Aileen Riggin, teenaged Olympic swimming and diving champion; Gertrude Ederle, the first woman to swim the English Channel; and Suzanne Lenglen, Helen Wills, and Molla Bjurstedt Mallory, three superb tennis players. One beloved athlete was not a person, but a horse! During his brief career, Man o' War triumphed in all but one of his races and became one of the most celebrated racehorses of the twentieth century.

Jack Dempsey (1895–1983) Boxer Jack Dempsey was nicknamed the "Manassa Mauler," for his hometown of Manassa, Colorado. In 1919, he knocked out Jess Willard (1881–1968) to become the heavyweight boxing champ. Then in 1926 and 1927, he fought two memorable title bouts against Gene Tunney (1897–1978). In his career, Dempsey won sixty of eighty bouts. His twenty nonvictories included six losses, eight draws, and six no-decisions. Fifty of his wins were by knockout, and half of these took place in the first round. *Photo reproduced by permission of Archive Photos, Inc.*

Lou Gehrig (1903–1941) At the beginning of his career, Lou Gehrig played in the shadow of Babe Ruth. In 1927, Gehrig smacked forty-seven home runs for the New York Yankees, while Ruth belted sixty. In the 1928 World Series, Gehrig hit .545 and Ruth hit .625. However, Gehrig is perhaps the greatest-ever major league first-baseman. During his career, he hit twenty-three grand slams (home runs with the bases loaded) and played in 2,130 straight games. He died at age thirty-seven of amyotrophic lateral sclerosis (ALS), a disease that attacks nerve cells in the brain and spinal cord. The illness came to be known as "Lou Gehrig's disease." *Photo reproduced by permission of Archive Photos, Inc.*

Harold "Red" Grange (1903–1991) Harold "Red" Grange, halfback for the University of Illinois, was the nation's leading rusher from 1923 to 1925. During the first twelve minutes of a 1924 contest against Michigan, he scored four times: on a 95-yard kickoff return; and on runs of 44, 56, and 67 yards. Later in the same game, he ran for another touchdown (this one was for a measly fifteen yards!) and even threw an 18-yard touchdown pass. The Illini won, 39 to 14. It was for good reason that Grange was nicknamed the "Galloping Ghost." *Photo reproduced by permission of the Pro Football Hall of Fame.*

Bobby Jones (1902–1971) During the 1920s, Bobby Jones, Walter Hagen (1892–1969), and Gene Sarazen (1902–1999) dominated the golfing world. Of the trio, however, Jones was the one who truly defined the era. What set him apart was that he was a master practitioner of the sport; he often has been dubbed the greatest golfer of all time. Jones's career lasted only fourteen years, during which he played in fifty-two tournaments. He won twenty-three, and was just twenty-eight years old when he retired from competition in 1930. *Photo reproduced by permission of Archive Photos, Inc.*

Ernie Nevers (1903–1976) Ernie Nevers was a giant among college football players during the 1920s. He played offense and defense and also kicked field goals at Stanford, where he earned eleven letters in four sports. In the 1925 Rose Bowl against Notre Dame, he rushed for 114 yards on thirty-four carries, even though casts recently had been removed from both his ankles. He went on to play professional football, baseball, and basketball. In 1929, playing for the NFL Chicago Cardinals, he scored forty points against the rival Chicago Bears. In 1962, *Sports Illustrated* named Nevers the greatest college football player of all time. *Photo reproduced by permission of the Corbis Corporation.*

Knute Rockne (1888–1931) As a Notre Dame undergraduate during the previous decade, Knute Rockne had enjoyed a stellar career on the gridiron. In one 1913 contest, a 35 to 13 victory against Army, Gus Dorais (1891–1954) and Rockne helped revolutionize the game, with Dorais throwing and Rockne catching passes. Upon graduation, Rockne became a Notre Dame chemistry teacher. In 1917, he was hired to coach the football team. From then until his death in a 1931 plane crash, he compiled a record of 103 and 12, with five ties. His winning percentage was an astounding .881. *Photo reproduced courtesy of the Library of Congress.*

Babe Ruth (1895–1948) In all of baseball history, no ballplayer has had more of an impact on the game than George Herman "Babe" Ruth. He began his major league career in 1914, as a pitcher for the Boston Red Sox. In 1916 and 1917, he was a twenty-game winner, and he might have enjoyed a Hall-of-Fame career as a pitcher but for his ability to belt a baseball. In 1918, Ruth began playing the outfield. During the 1920s, he smashed homer after homer, forever ending what had been known as baseball's "dead-ball era." His ball-yard feats rescued the sport in the aftermath of the 1919 Black Sox gambling scandal. *Photo reproduced courtesy of the Library of Congress.*

Bill Tilden (1893–1953) During the 1920s, Bill Tilden almost single-handedly popularized the sport of tennis among the masses. In 1920, Tilden became the first American to win the men's singles title at Wimbledon, England. He earned six consecutive U.S. Open championships from 1920 to 1925, and won the tournament again in 1929, at age thirty-six. Starting in 1920, he led the U.S. Davis Cup team to seven straight championships. In 1925, he won fifty-seven straight games. Tilden's six-foot height earned him the nickname "Big Bill." *Photo reproduced by permission of the Corbis Corporation.*

Topics in the News

❖ IS MAJOR LEAGUE BASEBALL AN ILLEGAL MONOPOLY?

Antitrust laws regulate American business and prevent individual companies from monopolizing the marketplace. Back in the mid-1910s, the Federal League, a new professional baseball league, briefly rivaled the American League (AL) and National League (NL) before folding. The Feds' Baltimore franchise filed a lawsuit against Major League Baseball, claiming that the AL and NL had plotted against the league. The suit alleged that the established leagues acted as a monopoly by plotting to purchase Federal League franchises and destroy the new operation. The Baltimore team argued that the AL and NL were a business. They maintained a schedule of games, featuring teams that traveled from city to city and state to state. Their players were paid employees, and the teams charged admission to watch them play. Thus, baseball constituted interstate commerce, and the AL and NL should be regulated by the 1890 Sherman Anti-Trust Act: a federal law restricting the power of the major business monopolies that emerged after the Civil War.

However, in 1922 the U.S. Supreme Court decreed that baseball was exempt from federal antitrust laws. Justice Oliver Wendell Holmes Jr. (1841–1935) noted that, in the view of the court, professional "exhibitions of baseball" did not constitute interstate commerce.

The ruling has been challenged several times over the decades: For example, in 1957, when professional football sought similar legal protection; in 1972, when Curt Flood (1938–1997), a veteran major league ballplayer, refused to accept his trade from the St. Louis Cardinals to the Philadelphia Phillies; and between the 2001 and 2002 seasons, when Commissioner Bud Selig (1934–) attempted to eliminate two major league franchises.

❖ BASEBALL: FROM THE BLACK SOX SCANDAL TO THE BABE

In 1919, the Chicago White Sox were heavily favored to beat the Cincinnati Reds in the World Series. However, the Reds came out on top. While it was neither the first nor the last upset victory in a major sporting event, the White Sox defeat was different because it was tainted.

During the last month of the 1920 season, certain members of the Sox were accused of accepting, or having had knowledge of, bribes from gamblers to throw the Series. Eight players were accused: outfielders Happy Felsch and "Shoeless" Joe Jackson; third baseman Buck Weaver; shortstop

Swede Risberg; first baseman Chick Gandil; pitchers Eddie Cicotte and Claude Williams; and utility infielder Fred McMullen. While a grand jury did not find the eight guilty as charged, the authorities banned them from baseball for life in order to restore public confidence in the game. One of the Black Sox, Jackson, was among the decade's top players. His banishment kept him from being elected to the Baseball Hall of Fame.

In order to re-establish the game's integrity, baseball team owners created the office of the commissioner to govern the sport and insure that no similar incidents would occur. The commissioner owed allegiance neither to the American League nor the National League. In 1921, Kenesaw Mountain Landis (1866–1944), a U.S. district court judge, was named to the office. He ruled with unlimited power until his death.

However, one man was responsible for revitalizing the sport: Babe Ruth (1895–1948), the beloved "Bambino" and the "Sultan of Swat." Ruth came to the major leagues during the previous decade as a pitcher for the Boston Red Sox. During the final week of 1919, team owner Harry Frazee (1881–1929) sold him to the New York Yankees for $100,000 and a $300,000 loan. During the 1910s, the Red Sox had won four World Series; in the decades after the trade, the team rarely advanced to the World

The 1919 Chicago White Sox baseball team which was heavily favored to beat the Cincinnati Reds in the World Series. Among the members are eight players accused of accepting, or having had knowledge of, bribes from gamblers to throw the Series. Reproduced courtesy of the National Baseball Hall of Fame and Museum.

Series and never emerged victorious. It was for this reason that the trade came to be regarded by baseball fans in general (and Red Sox loyalists in particular) as having inflicted on the team the "Curse of the Bambino."

In the years before 1919, in what was known as the "dead-ball era," major league home run totals generally were small. A player might lead his league in home runs by hitting eight, nine, or twelve pitches out of the ballpark. Frank Baker (1886–1963), a future Hall of Famer who earned the nickname "Home Run," never hit more than twelve in a season. During his thirteen-year major league career, his homer total was ninety-six. Yet in 1919, Ruth astounded the baseball world by hitting twenty-nine homers. The following year, he smashed fifty-four, a number that exceeded all the totals for every major league team but the Philadelphia Phillies. Midway through the 1921 season, Ruth belted his 137th homer, breaking the career record of nineteenth-century star Roger Connor (1857–1931). Ruth finished the season with fifty-nine homers, and led the Yankees to their first-ever World Series appearance. Back then, the NL's New York Giants were the powerhouse of New York baseball. Managed by confrontational, charismatic John McGraw (1873–1934), the Giants made World Series appearances in 1905, 1911, 1912, 1913, and 1917. In both 1921 and 1922, the Giants and Yankees faced each other. Both times, the Giants emerged victorious. When the teams met again in 1923, the Yankees won. That year was the team's first in their new home: Yankee Stadium, which quickly became known as "the house that Ruth built."

Dozens of baseball legends played in the major leagues during the decade. Among them were New York Yankee first baseman Lou Gehrig (1903–1941), who began his streak of 2,130 consecutive games played in 1925; Rogers Hornsby (1896–1963), who hit over .400 three times and won the Triple Crown in 1922 and 1925 by leading the NL in home runs, runs batted in (RBIs), and batting average; Jimmy Foxx (1907–1967), one of baseball's top sluggers, who totaled 534 homers during his career; George Sisler (1893–1973), who hit .407, .371, and .420 from 1920 to 1922; and Tris Speaker (1888–1958), who hit over .375 six times. However, no other ballplayer was as colorful as George Herman "Babe" Ruth. No other ballplayer was as commanding as Ruth. No other ballplayer so shaped and influenced the game.

❖ THE NEW YORK YANKEES

Throughout the twentieth century, the New York Yankees were major league baseball's most successful franchise. Arguably, the 1927 Yankees were the best of all New York teams and one of the greatest ever to play the national pastime.

Year	Winning Team	Losing Team
1920	Cleveland Indians (AL) 5	Brooklyn Dodgers (NL) 2
1921	New York Giants (NL) 5	New York Yankees (AL) 3
1922	New York Giants (NL) 4	New York Yankees (AL) 0
1923	New York Yankees (AL) 4	New York Giants (NL) 2
1924	Washington Senators (AL) 4	New York Giants (NL) 3
1925	Pittsburgh Pirates (NL) 4	Washington Senators (AL) 3
1926	St. Louis Cardinals (NL) 4	New York Yankees (AL) 3
1927	New York Yankees (AL) 4	Pittsburgh Pirates (NL) 0
1928	New York Yankees (AL) 4	St. Louis Cardinals (NL) 0
1929	Philadelphia Athletics (AL) 4	Chicago Cubs (NL) 1

The '27 Yankees were nicknamed "Murderer's Row." They finished the season with a 110 and 44 record. The team batting average was .307. Its slugging percentage was .498, a major league record. Babe Ruth smashed sixty home runs, a record that would stand until 1961 when a future Yankee, Roger Maris (1934–1985), would hit sixty-one. As a team, the '27 Yanks hit 158 home runs, 102 more than the team with the second-highest total. In addition to his sixty homers, Ruth compiled a .356 batting average and drove in 164 runs. Lou Gehrig hit .373, and drove in 175 runs. Six pitchers won at least ten games. The pitching staff compiled an earned-run average (ERA) of 3.20; the next-best club's ERA was 3.91.

The '27 Yankees swept the Pittsburgh Pirates in the World Series. They did the same the following season against the St. Louis Cardinals. It was the first time one team had swept two consecutive World Series, and it signaled the start of Yankees postseason domination for decades to come.

❖ THE NEGRO LEAGUES ALSO PROVIDE EXCITING PLAY

In the 1920s, African Americans were excluded from playing major league baseball. It was not until 1947 that Jackie Robinson (1919–1972) became the first of his race to join a major league ball club during the twentieth century. African Americans did play professionally, however, in what collectively were known as the Negro Leagues.

While all-black baseball teams dated to the nineteenth century, they remained unorganized in the early twentieth century. Then in 1920, Andrew "Rube" Foster (1879–1930), the "father of black baseball," established the eight-team Negro National League, the first structured black league. Earlier, Foster had pitched for and managed the Chicago American Giants, a successful all-black team. The Negro National League was an immediate success: in 1923, it attracted over four hundred thousand fans. Then a conglomeration of white owners set up a second league, the Eastern Colored League, consisting of six teams. In 1924, the pennant-winning teams from both leagues met in the first black World Series. The Negro National League's Kansas City Monarchs won, beating the Philadelphia Hilldales five games to four.

Dozens of exemplary ballplayers starred in the Negro Leagues. Those who played during the 1920s included Oscar Charleston (1896–1954), arguably the greatest all-around Negro League player; Leroy "Satchel" Paige (1906–1982), a legendary pitcher and the leagues' premier draw; Bill Foster

Legendary pitcher Leroy "Satchel" Paige was just one of the dozens of exemplary ballplayers that starred in the Negro Leagues. *Reproduced by permission of AP/Wide World Photos.*

(1904–1978), Rube's half-brother, a top hurler; William "Judy" Johnson (1899–1989), a steady third-baseman and expert contact hitter; Wilbur "Bullet" Rogan (1889–1967), a brainy pitcher and outfielder; John Henry "Pop" Lloyd (1884–1965), the best-ever Negro League shortstop; James "Cool Papa" Bell (1903–1991), a lightning-fast base-stealer; Martin Dihigo (1905–1971), who played all nine positions; and Willie Wells (1906–1989), a power-hitting shortstop. Sturdy first-baseman Walter "Buck" Leonard (1907–1997) and slugging catcher Josh Gibson (1911–1947) were two future Negro League greats. Occasionally, Negro League players squared off against, and played as well as, their white major league counterparts.

Jackie Robinson's integration of the majors proved catastrophic for the Negro Leagues, which ceased to exist during the 1950s as more and more young black ballplayers signed with American and National League ball clubs.

❖ BASKETBALL

Throughout the 1920s, basketball primarily was an amateur sport, played on college campuses. Even then, school teams mostly competed solely within their regions. There were no major nationally known basketball stars to rival those in college football, and no single team dominated the sport.

Concurrently, efforts to establish professional basketball leagues were unsuccessful. One of the more enterprising attempts was the American Basketball League, formed in 1925, which folded in the 1930s. The decade's major professional team was the Original Celtics (not to be confused with the Boston Celtics), which had been formed in New York before World War I. The team had no league in which to play, so it barnstormed across the country taking on local and amateur squads. Celtic players were the first to be signed to individual contracts instead of being paid on a game-by-game basis. As a result, they were able to gel as a team. Players could concentrate on honing their individual skills and working together to develop on-court offensive and defensive strategies. Usually, the Celtics won 90 percent of their games. During the 1922 and 1923 season, they compiled a 204 and 11 record.

During this period, neither professional nor college teams featured African American players. In 1927, Abe Saperstein (1901–1966), a businessman and promoter, formed the Harlem Globetrotters, an all-black team. Initially, the Globetrotters regularly walloped the competition. They eventually evolved into a troupe of entertainers who combined athletic skill with flashy passing, jumping, and dribbling. Supposedly, Saperstein added physical comedy to the Globetrotters' act to entertain fans who were tiring of the team's customary, one-sided victories.

❖ BOXING: A DECADE OF STARS

Jack Dempsey (1895–1983), who defeated Jess Willard (1881–1968) in 1919 to win the heavyweight title, was perhaps the 1920s' most compelling boxer. His two greatest fights were both against Gene Tunney (1897–1978), another dominating heavyweight. After beating Willard, Dempsey knocked out all challengers: Billy Miske and Bill Brennan in 1920; George Carpentier in 1921; and Tom Gibbons and Luis Firpo in 1923. Then in 1926, he was defeated by Tunney. By then, boxing had become overwhelmingly popular. When Dempsey took the title from Willard, he did so before 19,650 fans at the Bay View Park Arena in Toledo, Ohio. By contrast, the official attendance at the first Dempsey-Tunney bout, held at Sesquicentennial Stadium in Philadelphia, was 120,757.

The rematch, held exactly one year later at Chicago's Soldier Field before 104,943 fans, became one of the twentieth century's legendary title fights. It was dubbed "the battle of the Long Count" because of a determination by the referee that Dempsey failed to return to a neutral corner after knocking down Tunney in the seventh round. Because of Dempsey's negligence, the referee delayed the count. Tunney got up at the official count of "nine," which was estimated to really have been "fourteen." He eventually beat Dempsey in a ten-round decision and in 1928 retired with his championship intact.

Benny Leonard (1896–1947), a powerhouse fighter, was lightweight boxing champion from 1917 to 1924, at which point he retired. He mounted a comeback after losing his life savings in the 1929 stock market crash. Fighting as a welterweight, he won nineteen bouts before stepping aside permanently in 1932. It has been said that, pound for pound, Leonard was the toughest fighter who ever lived.

Tex Rickard (1870–1929), a shrewd promoter, was responsible for increasing the winnings of the top boxers and bringing glamour and prestige to their bouts. In 1921, Rickard staged the first boxing match to draw $1 million at the gate: the heavyweight title fight pitting Jack Dempsey against Frenchman George Carpentier (1894–1975). The bout also was the first to be aired on radio. For the second Dempsey-Tunney fight, the gate topped over $2.6 million. Tunney's cut was a record $990,445.

❖ COLLEGE FOOTBALL'S GLORY DAYS

During the 1920s, the popularity of college football skyrocketed to dizzying heights. Schools constructed huge steel-and-concrete stadiums which seated seventy thousand or more cheering students and football diehards. If Harold "Red" Grange (1903–1991) of the University of Illinois

and Ernie Nevers (1903–1976) of Stanford were the most celebrated college grid stars, the one team that dominated throughout the decade was Notre Dame, coached by the legendary Knute Rockne (1888–1931). Until the 1920s, most college football teams had played only regional rivals. However, under Rockne, Notre Dame competed against the best teams across the country. A string of illustrious athletes played under Rockne. Few were more famous than the 1924 backfield, nicknamed "The Four Horsemen of the Apocalypse." They won this nickname after sportswriter Grantland Rice (1880–1954) saw them perform against Army. "Outlined against the blue-gray October sky," Rice wrote, "the Four Horsemen rode again. In dramatic lore they were known as famine, pestilence, destruction, and death. These are only aliases. Their real names are Stuhldreher, Miller, Crowley, and Layden." Another Notre Dame all-American earned immortality for an alleged off-the-field declaration. Fullback George Gipp (1895–1920) became fatally ill during the 1920 season. While on his deathbed, legend has it that he told his coach, "Sometime, Rock, when the team is up against it, when things are wrong and the breaks are beating the boys, ask them to win one for the Gipper."

Among the many memorable Notre Dame games during the decade was a 27 to 10 victory in the 1925 Rose Bowl over Stanford, with the Four Horseman pitted against Nevers. Other teams also enjoyed success, however. One was Stanford, which in 1926 played Alabama to a 7 to 7 Rose Bowl tie. The teams emerged as conational champions.

❖ PROFESSIONAL FOOTBALL GETS OFF THE GROUND

Prior to the 1920s, pro football was a disorganized, disreputable enterprise. Most teams

National Football League Champions

Year	College
1921	Chicago Staleys (Bears)
1922	Canton Bulldogs
1923	Canton Bulldogs
1924	Cleveland Bulldogs
1925	Chicago Cardinals
1926	Frankford Yellowjackets
1927	New York Giants
1928	Providence Steamrollers
1929	Green Bay Packers

were located in Pennsylvania, Ohio, and the Chicago, Illinois area; players often switched teams during seasons; and gambling scandals were frequent. Not surprisingly, fans preferred college football.

In order to improve the image of pro football and increase profitability, representatives from several Ohio teams met at a Hupmobile car agency showroom in Canton, Ohio, in 1920. Emerging from this meeting and a subsequent gathering was the American Professional Football Association (APFA). The league's goal was to raise "the standard of professional football...eliminate bidding for players...[and] secure cooperation in the formation of schedules, at least for the bigger teams." Fourteen teams competed during the inaugural season. With the exception of two teams from New York (the Buffalo All-Americans and the Rochester Jeffersons), all were from the Midwest: Akron Pros; Canton Bulldogs; Chicago Tigers; Cleveland Tigers/Indians; Columbus Panhandles; Dayton Triangles; Decatur Staleys; Detroit Heralds; Hammond Pros; Muncie Flyers; Racine (Chicago) Cardinals; and Rock Island Independents. At the end of the 1920 season, the Association changed its name to the one familiar to present-day football fans: the National Football League (NFL).

Most teams lasted a season or two before folding. The Green Bay Packers joined the league in 1921, and almost suffered the same fate the following season. The Packers' demise was avoided when local Green Bay businessmen established a public, nonprofit corporation to run the team. Back then, a fan

OPPOSITE PAGE
Notre Dame football player George Gipp became famous for his alleged deathbed request "...win one for the Gipper." Reproduced by permission of Archive Photos, Inc.

could purchase a share in the team, along with a season ticket, for the princely sum of $5! By the end of the twentieth century, the Packers were valued at more than $150 million and remained a publicly held franchise.

Of the original league franchises, only two survived throughout the twentieth century. One was the Decatur Staleys. A year after the league's inception, the Staleys moved to Chicago. In 1929, the team name was changed to the Chicago Bears. The other was the Racine Cardinals. Actually, from the outset, the team was located in Chicago; the "Racine" referred to a Chicago street, rather than the Wisconsin city. During the 1920 season, the team became the Chicago Cardinals. That franchise relocated to St. Louis, Missouri, in 1960 and to Arizona in 1988.

❖ FOOTBALL'S FAMOUS PAPA BEAR

George Halas (1895–1983), a player, coach, team owner, and league founder, is one of the blocks of granite at the foundation of the NFL. At the league's outset, Halas represented the Decatur Staleys. He played left end on the team and also was its coach and business manager. He remained the franchise's coach (intermittently) through 1967.

During its early years, the NFL was floundering. Most college stars disregarded the infant league, which was in urgent need of a gate attraction. Halas was responsible for winning credibility for the NFL when, in 1925, he signed college gridiron star Harold "Red" Grange" (1903–1991) to play for the Staleys. Grange became the NFL's initial superstar. His first game out of college drew a standing-room-only crowd of thirty-six thousand spectators to Chicago's Wrigley Field; seventy-three thousand fans showed up when the Staleys went to New York City's Polo Grounds to play the Giants. It was the largest crowd ever to attend a pro football game. Ernie Nevers (1903–1976) followed Grange to the NFL, signing a contract with the Duluth Eskimos the following season.

Halas's other innovations included instituting daily practices, signing radio broadcast contracts, covering the playing field with a tarpaulin when it was not in use, and employing a public address system to inform fans which player had just carried the ball, who had made the tackle, and how much yardage was needed for a first down. He also understood the importance of employing top assistant coaches who were experts in their respective specialties. It was for good reason that Halas earned the nickname "Papa Bear."

❖ GOLF'S WIDENING APPEAL

While not as wildly popular as major league baseball, pro boxing, and college football, golf enjoyed a surge in interest during the 1920s. Between

U.S. Golf Association Open Champions

Year	Player
1920	Edward "Ted" Ray
1921	Jim Barnes
1922	Gene Sarazen
1923	Bobby Jones
1924	Cyril Walker
1925	Willie MacFarlane
1926	Bobby Jones
1927	Tommy Armour
1928	John Farrell
1929	Bobby Jones

1916 and 1920, the number of weekend golfers doubled across the country. New courses, both public and private, were constructed. Previously, golf had been the domain of the well-to-do. Now, those in the middle class were enjoying the sport both as participants and spectators.

Three golfers dominated the sport: Bobby Jones (1902–1971); Walter Hagen (1892–1969); and Gene Sarazen (1902–1999). Together, they were dubbed the Three Musketeers; no other golfer, foreign or American, matched them in competition. Jones simply was a master golfer. He won thirteen major titles: four U.S. Opens, three British Opens, five U.S. Amateurs, and one British Amateur. In 1926, he became the first golfer to win the U.S. Open and British Open during the same year. The feat earned him a ticker-tape parade in New York City. Then in 1930, Jones won the British Amateur, British Open, U.S. Open, and U.S. Amateur. Afterwards, he retired from competition. In 1950, an Associated Press poll judged the feat "the supreme athletic achievement of the century."

Unlike many golfers of the period, who came from comfortable backgrounds, Sarazen grew up in poverty. He became the first player ever to win all four Grand Slam titles: the Masters; the U.S. Open; the British Open (which he won twice); and the PGA Championship (which he won three times). The third Musketeer, the likable, outgoing Hagen, was fondly nick-

Kentucky Derby Winners[1]

Year	Horse
1920	Paul Jones
1921	Behave Yourself
1922	Morvich
1923	Zev
1924	Black Gold
1925	Flying Ebony
1926	Bubbling Over
1927	Whiskery
1928	Reigh Count
1929	Clyde Van Dusen

named "The Haig." He won his first U.S. Open in 1914, and was the British Open champ in 1922, 1924, 1928, and 1929; his 1922 victory was the first by an American-born golfer. Hagen also was the Professional Golfers' Association (PGA) champion for four consecutive years, beginning in 1924.

❖ HORSERACING'S HERO: MAN O' WAR

Before the rise of Man o' War, horseracing was viewed in many circles either as an amusement for the rich or a temptation for those corrupted by gambling. However, this powerful and apparently unbeatable horse single-handedly helped popularize and make reputable yet another sport among the masses.

Man o' War, a son of Fair Play, was foaled in Kentucky and sold as a yearling for five thousand dollars. Nicknamed Big Red for his deep chestnut color, the colt won an astounding twenty of twenty-one races in 1919 and 1920, when he was two and three years old. He suffered his lone defeat in August 1919, at the Sanford Stakes in Saratoga, New York. The winning horse had a most appropriate name: Upset.

While Man o' War was not entered into the Kentucky Derby, the horse did win the other two legs of the Triple Crown: the Preakness and the Belmont Stakes. In July 1920, Man o' War took on John P. Grier in the Dewey Stakes at New York's Aqueduct track in what is regarded as one of the great races in the sport's history. The horses ran neck-and-neck for most of the race, with Man o' War finally forging ahead. He not only won by almost two lengths but also set a new world record of one minute and 49.12 seconds for a mile-and-one-sixteenth course.

In the final contest of his career, Man o' War easily defeated Sir Barton, the 1919 Triple Crown winner, in a match race. Man o' War retired as the sport's leading money winner, totaling a then-record $249,465.

❖ THE OLYMPIC GAMES SHINE

With the world finally at peace after the horror of the recently concluded Great War (1914–18; also known as World War I), the 1920s saw three Olympics Games held, all in Western Europe. Antwerp, Belgium, was the site of the first contest in 1920. This small European country was so honored because of the courage its citizens had displayed during the war. Unfortunately, Belgium was not a wise selection because insufficient finances were available to construct adequate facilities for the games. In any case, with the war having just ended, most nations fielded under-trained teams. However, the 1920s Olympics were noteworthy as the first in which American women were allowed to compete, and the first featuring the famous five-ring Olympic flag. In 1924, the games were held in Paris in honor of Baron de Coubertin (1863–1937), retiring chairman of the International Olympic Committee (IOC). That year also saw the debut of the Winter Olympics, held in Chamonix, France. Four years later Amsterdam, the Netherlands, hosted the summer games. These Olympics were the first in which women competed in track-and-field events, and the first in which an Olympic flame burned throughout the games. In 1928, the second Winter Olympics were held in St. Moritz, Switzerland.

Numerous Olympic legends starred during the decade. In 1920, Aileen Riggin was just past her fourteenth birthday when she won the diving competition, making her the youngest female gold medalist in history. Four years later, she won medals in swimming and diving and continued swimming competitively into the 1990s, when she was in her nineties. Also in 1920, Charley Paddock (1900–1943) became the first of several athletes throughout the twentieth century to earn the title "world's fastest human" when he won the 100-meter dash. That year, Hawaii's Duke Kahanamoku (1890–1968), a fabled swimmer and surfer, set an Olympic swimming record of 1:01.4 seconds in the 100-meter freestyle.

In 1926, Gertrude Ederle became the first woman to swim the English Channel. **Reproduced by permission of Archive Photos, Inc.**

Two athletes dominated the 1924 games: Paavo Nurmi (1897–1973), the Flying Finn, a distance runner who won four events; and swimmer Johnny Weissmuller (1904–1984), who claimed three gold medals. Weissmuller won another in 1928. Then he retired from athletic competition and during the 1930s, he became Hollywood's most famous Tarzan. The 1924 games featured upset victories by Harold Abrahams (1899–1978), a Jewish student at Cambridge, in the 100-meter race, and Eric Liddell (1902–1945), a devout Scottish missionary, in the 400-meter race. Their

U.S. Open Tennis Singles Champions

Year	Male Winner	Female Winner
1920	Bill Tilden	Molla Bjurdstedt Mallory
1921	Bill Tilden	Molla Bjurdstedt Mallory
1922	Bill Tilden	Molla Bjurdstedt Mallory
1923	Bill Tilden	Helen Wills
1924	Bill Tilden	Helen Wills
1925	Bill Tilden	Helen Wills
1926	René Lacoste	Molla Bjurdstedt Mallory
1927	René Lacoste	Helen Wills
1928	Henri Cochet	Helen Wills
1929	Bill Tilden	Helen Wills

stories are recounted in the Academy Award-winning film *Chariots of Fire* (1981). Also in 1924, swimmer Gertrude Ederle (1906–) came away with one gold and two bronze medals. In 1926, she became the first woman to swim the English Channel.

❖ TENNIS

During the 1920s, Bill Tilden (1893–1953) became the first tennis player to earn national renown, winning seven U.S. Open titles and three championships at Wimbledon in England. Tilden was noted for his power game, which consisted of hard serves and ground strokes. His dramatic play helped secure popularity for yet another sport that previously had been considered the exclusive domain of the wealthy. Tilden's one nemesis, however, was a Frenchman, René Lacoste (1905–1996). In 1927, Tilden was beating Lacoste in the French Open before he faltered and lost. Later that year, Lacoste defeated him again in the U.S. Open. Lacoste himself won seven major singles titles.

Women also dominated the sport. France's Suzanne Lenglen (1899–1938), nicknamed the "French Goddess," brought attention to women's tennis both for her exceptional game and for the clothing she wore in competition. Previously, women players were modestly attired, playing in long, often heavy dresses. Lenglen wore clothing that exposed her ankles and forearms, which was considered quite shocking. She also broke another taboo by showing emotion on the court, and she even took sips of brandy between sets. Among her accomplishments during the decade were five straight Wimbledon titles.

Lenglen's American counterpart was Helen Wills (1905–1998). Unlike Lenglen, Wills played without emotion; she even earned the nickname "Little Miss Poker Face." Wills had just won three straight U.S. Open titles when, in 1926, she faced off against Lenglen while touring through France. The two met at the Carlton Club, a small country club in Cannes, and Lenglen emerged victorious. It was the only time they competed. Despite this defeat, Wills won an astounding eight Wimbledon crowns and thirty-one major titles.

A third woman starred in the sport during the decade: Molla Bjurstedt Mallory (1884–1959). In 1921, in the second round of the U.S. Open, Mallory defeated Lenglen. It was the latter's only defeat as an amateur.

 For More Information

BOOKS

Allen, Maury. *Big-Time Baseball: A Complete Record of the National Sport.* New York: Hart Publishing Company, 1978.

Bacho, Peter. *Boxing in Black and White.* New York: Henry Holt, 1999.

Carroll, Bob, Michael Gershman, David Neff, and John Thorn, eds. *Total Football II.* New York: HarperCollins, 1999.

Christopher, Matt. *Great Moments in Baseball History.* Boston: Little Brown & Company, 1996

Diamond, Dan, Ralph Dinger, and James Duplacey, eds. *Total Hockey.* Kingston, NY: Total Sports, 1998.

Edelman, Rob. *Great Baseball Films.* New York: Citadel Press, 1994.

Falla, Jack, ed. *Quest for the Cup: A History of the Stanley Cup Finals, 1893–2001.* San Diego: Thunder Bay Press, 2001.

Flink, Steven. *The Greatest Tennis Matches of the Twentieth Century.* Danbury, CT: Rutledge Books, 1999.

Gilbert, Thomas. *The Soaring Twenties: Babe Ruth and the Home-Run Decade.* New York: Franklin Watts, 1996.

Greenspan, Bud. *100 Greatest Moments in Olympic History.* Los Angeles: General Publishing Group, 1995.

Greenspan, Bud, and Zander Hollander, eds. *Bud Collins' Modern Encyclopedia of Tennis, Second Edition.* Detroit: Visible Ink Press, 1993.

Heinz, W.C., and Nathan Ward, eds. *The Book of Boxing.* New York: Total Sports, 1999.

Heisler, John, and Knute Rockne. *Quotable Rockne.* Nashville, TN: TowleHouse Publishers, 2001.

Jacobs, William Jay. *They Shaped the Game: Ty Cobb, Babe Ruth, Jackie Robinson.* New York: Charles Scribner's Sons, 1994.

Kavanagh, Jack. *Shoeless Joe Jackson.* New York: Chelsea House, 1995.

McKissack, Patricia, and Frederick McKissack, Jr. *Black Diamond: The Story of the Negro Baseball Leagues.* New York: Scholastic Trade, 1994.

Riley, James A. *The Negro Leagues.* New York: Chelsea House, 1996.

Ritter, Lawrence. *The Story of Baseball.* New York: Morrow Junior Books, 1999.

Savage, Jeff. *Home Run Kings.* Austin, TX: Raintree/Steck-Vaughn, 1999.

Stewart, Mark. *Baseball: A History of the National Pastime.* New York: Franklin Watts, 1998.

Stewart, Mark. *Football: A History of the Gridiron Game.* New York: Franklin Watts, 1998.

Thorn, John, Pete Palmer, and Michael Gershman, eds. *Total Baseball, Seventh Edition.* Kingston, NY: Total Sports, 2001.

Whittingham, Richard. *Rites of Autumn: The Story of College Football.* New York: Free Press, 2001.

WEB SITES

Major Sporting Events of the 1920s. http://din-timelines.com/1920s-sport.shtml (accessed on August 5, 2002).

New York Yankees History. http://newyork.yankees.mlb.com/NASApp/mlb/nyy/history/nyy_history_timeline.jsp?period=1 (accessed on August 5, 2002).

The 1920s: Sports and Players of the 1920s. http://www.louisville.edu/~kprayb01/1920s-Sports.html (accessed on August 2, 2002).

Where to Learn More

BOOKS

Allen, Frederick Lewis. *America Transforms Itself: 1900–1950*. New Brunswick, NJ: Transaction Pub., 1993.

Allen, Frederick Lewis. *Only Yesterday: An Informal History of the 1920s*. New York: Perennial Classics, 2000.

Allen, Maury. *Big-Time Baseball: A Complete Record of the National Sport*. New York: Hart Publishing Company, 1978.

Altman Linda Jacobs. *The Decade That Roared: America During Prohibition*. New York: Twenty-First Century Books, 1997.

Andryszewski, Tricia. *Immigration: Newcomers and Their Impact on the United States*. Brookfield, CT: Millbrook Press, 1995.

Andryszewski, Tricia. *School Prayer: A History of the Debate*. Springfield, NJ: Enslow Publishers, 1997.

Applebaum, Stanley, ed. *The New York Stage: Famous Productions in Photographs*. New York: Dover Publications, 1976.

Bacho, Peter. *Boxing in Black and White*. New York: Henry Holt, 1999.

Bachrach, Deborah. *The Importance of Margaret Sanger*. San Diego: Lucent Books, 1993.

Barr, Roger. *Radio: Wireless Sound*. San Diego: Lucent Books, 1994.

Berry, Michael. *Georgia O'Keeffe*. New York: Chelsea House, 1988.

Bloom, Harold, ed. *Ernest Hemingway*. Philadelphia: Chelsea House, 2001.

Bloom, Harold, ed. *F. Scott Fitzgerald*. Philadelphia: Chelsea House, 2000.

Bloom, Harold, ed. *James Joyce*. Philadelphia: Chelsea House, 2001.

Blum, Daniel. *Great Stars of the American Stage.* New York: Grosset & Dunlap, 1952.

Blum, Daniel. *A Pictorial History of the American Theatre,* 6th ed. New York: Crown Publishers, 1986.

Blum, Daniel. *A Pictorial History of the Silent Screen.* New York: Putnam, 1953.

Bolden, Tonya, ed. *33 Things Every Girl Should Know About Women's History: From Suffragettes to Skirt Lengths to the E.R.A.* New York: Crown Publishing, 2002.

Brennan, Kristine. *The Stock Market Crash of 1929.* Philadelphia: Chelsea House, 2000.

Buxton, Frank, and Bill Owen. *The Big Broadcast, 1920–1950.* New York: The Viking Press, 1966.

Candaele, Kerry. *Bound for Glory 1910–1930: From the Great Migration to the Harlem Renaissance.* New York: Chelsea House, 1996.

Carroll, Bob, Michael Gershman, David Neff, and John Thorn, eds. *Total Football II.* New York: HarperCollins, 1999.

Cefrey, Holly. *Syphilis and Other Sexually Transmitted Diseases.* New York: Rosen Publishing Group, 2002.

Chant, Christopher. *Famous Trains of the 20th Century.* Philadelphia: Chelsea House, 2000.

Christopher, Matt. *Great Moments in Baseball History.* Boston: Little Brown & Company, 1996

Clinton, Susan. *Herbert Hoover.* Chicago: Children's Press, 1988.

Collins, David R. *Bix Beiderbecke: Jazz Age Genius.* Greensboro, NC: Morgan Reynolds, 1998.

Daffron, Carolyn. *Edna St. Vincent Millay.* New York: Chelsea House, 1989.

Datnow, Claire L. *Edwin Hubble: Discoverer of Galaxies.* Springfield, NJ: Enslow Publishers, 1997.

Denenberg, Barry. *An American Hero: The True Story of Charles A. Lindbergh.* New York: Scholastic, 1996.

Denzel, Justin F. *Genius With a Scalpel: Harvey Cushing.* New York: Messner, 1971.

Diamond, Dan, Ralph Dinger, and James Duplacey, eds. *Total Hockey.* Kingston, NY: Total Sports, 1998.

Dolan, Terrance. *Probing Deep Space.* New York: Chelsea House, 1993.

Edelman, Rob. *Great Baseball Films.* New York: Citadel Press, 1994.

Falla, Jack, ed. *Quest for the Cup: A History of the Stanley Cup Finals, 1893–2001.* San Diego: Thunder Bay Press, 2001.

Feinberg, Barbara Silberdick. *Black Tuesday: The Stock Market Crash of 1929.* Brookfield, CT: Millbrook Press, 1995.

Feinstein, Stephen. *The 1920s: From Prohibition to Charles Lindbergh.* Berkeley Heights, NJ: Enslow Publishers, 2001.

Ferber, Elizabeth. *Diabetes.* Brookfield, CT: Millbrook Press, 1996.

Feuerlicht, Roberta Strauss. *America's Reign of Terror: World War I, the Red Scare, and the Palmer Raids.* New York: Random House, 1971.

Finkelstein, Norman H. *Sounds in the Air: The Golden Age of Radio.* New York: Atheneum, 1993.

Flink, Steven. *The Greatest Tennis Matches of the Twentieth Century.* Danbury, CT: Rutledge Books, 1999.

Fox, Mary Virginia. *Edwin Hubble: American Astronomer.* New York: Franklin Watts, 1997.

Freedman, Russell. *Martha Graham: A Dancer's Life.* New York: Clarion, 1998.

Funk, Gary D. *A Balancing Act: Sports and Education.* Minneapolis: Lerner Publications Company, 1995.

Galbraith, John Kenneth. *The Great Crash: 1929.* Boston: Houghton Mifflin, 1997 (reprint edition).

Gay, Kathlyn. *Who's Running the Nation? How Corporate Power Threatens Democracy.* New York: Franklin Watts, 1998.

Giblin, James. *Charles A. Lindbergh: A Human Hero.* New York: Clarion Books, 1997.

Gilbert, Thomas. *The Soaring Twenties: Babe Ruth and the Home-Run Decade.* New York: Franklin Watts, 1996.

Gottfried, Ted. *The American Media.* New York: Franklin Watts, 1997.

Greenspan, Bud, and Zander Hollander, eds. *Bud Collins' Modern Encyclopedia of Tennis,* 2nd ed. Detroit: Visible Ink Press, 1993.

Greenspan, Bud. *100 Greatest Moments in Olympic History.* Los Angeles: General Publishing Group, 1995

Grierson, John. *I Remember Lindbergh.* New York: Harcourt Brace, 1977.

Halliwell, Sarah, ed. *The 20th Century: Pre–1945 Artists, Writers, and Composers.* Austin, TX: Raintree/Steck-Vaughn, 1998.

Hanson, Erica. *The 1920s.* San Diego, CA: Lucent Books, 1999.

Hanson, Freya Ottem. *The Scopes Monkey Trial: A Headline Court Case.* Berkeley Heights, NJ: Enslow Publishers, 2000.

Hardy, P. Stephen, and Sheila Jackson Hardy. *Extraordinary People of the Harlem Renaissance.* New York: Children's Press, 2000.

Haskins, James. *The Harlem Renaissance.* Brookfield, CT: Millbrook Press, 1996.

Heinz, W. C., and Nathan Ward, eds. *The Book of Boxing.* New York: Total Sports, 1999.

Heisler, John, and Knute Rockne. *Quotable Rockne.* Nashville, TN: TowleHouse Publishers, 2001.

Herald, Jacqueline. *Fashions of a Decade: The 1920s.* New York: Facts on File, 1991.

Hesse, Karen. *Witness.* New York: Scholastic Trade, 2001.

Hill, Christine. *Langston Hughes: Poet of the Harlem Renaissance.* Springfield, NJ: Enslow Publishers, 1997.

Hintz, Martin. *Farewell, John Barleycorn: Prohibition in the United States.* Minneapolis: Lerner Publications, 1996.

Holford, David M. *Herbert Hoover.* Berkeley Heights, NJ: Enslow Publishers, 1999.

Holt, Rackham. *Mary McLeod Bethune: A Biography.* Garden City, NY: Doubleday, 1964.

Hyde, Margaret O. *Know About Tuberculosis.* New York: Walker & Company, 1994.

Hyde, Margaret O., and Elizabeth H. Forsyth, MD. *Vaccinations: From Smallpox to Cancer.* New York: Franklin Watts, 2000.

Jacobs, Francine. *Breakthrough, the True Story of Penicillin.* New York: Dodd, Mead, 1985.

Jacobs, William Jay. *They Shaped the Game: Ty Cobb, Babe Ruth, Jackie Robinson.* New York: Charles Scribner's Sons, 1994.

Jacques, Geoffrey. *Free Within Ourselves: The Harlem Renaissance.* New York: Franklin Watts, 1996.

Janson, H.W., and Anthony F. Janson. *History of Art for Young People,* 5th ed. New York: Harry Abrams, 1997.

Katz, Ephraim. *The Film Encyclopedia,* 4th ed. New York: HarperResource, 2001.

Katz, William Loren. *The New Freedom to the New Deal, 1913–1939.* Austin, TX: Raintree/Steck-Vaughn, 1993.

Kavanagh, Jack. *Shoeless Joe Jackson.* New York: Chelsea House, 1995.

Kent, Zachary. *Charles Lindbergh and the Spirit of St. Louis in American History.* Berkeley Heights, NJ: Enslow Publishers, 2001.

Kreuger, Miles. *Show Boat: The Story of a Classic American Musical.* New York: Applause, 1995.

Landau, Elaine. *Diabetes.* New York: Twenty-First Century Books, 1994.

Landau, Elaine. *Tuberculosis.* New York: Franklin Watts, 1995.

Lawrence, Jerome, and Robert E. Lee. *Inherit the Wind.* New York: Dramatists Play Service, 2000. (reissue)

Lucas, Eileen. *The Eighteenth and Twenty-First Amendments: Alcohol-Prohibition and Repeal.* Springfield, NJ: Enslow Publishers, 1998.

Lutz, Norma Jean. *Battling the Klan.* Ulrichsville, OH: Barbour & Company, 1998.

Maltin, Leonard, ed. *The Great American Broadcast.* New York: Dutton, 1997.

Maltin, Leonard, ed. *Leonard Maltin's Movie Encyclopedia.* New York: Dutton, 1994.

Mark, Joan. *Margaret Mead: Coming of Age in America.* New York: Oxford University Press, 1999.

Matuz, Roger. *Albert Kahn: Architect of Detroit.* Detroit: Wayne State University Press, 2001.

Maurer, Richard. *Rocket! How a Toy Launched the Space Age.* New York: Crown Publishers, 1995.

McCarthy, Pat. *Henry Ford: Building Cars for Everyone.* Berkeley Heights, NJ: Enslow Publishers, 2002.

McKissack, Patricia, and Frederick McKissack, Jr. *Black Diamond: The Story of the Negro Baseball Leagues.* New York: Scholastic Trade, 1994.

Meachum, Virginia. *Charles Lindbergh: American Hero of Flight.* Berkeley Heights, NJ: Enslow Publishers, 2002.

Meltzer, Milton. *Brother, Can You Spare a Dime?: The Great Depression, 1929–1933.* New York, Facts on File, 1991 (reprint edition).

Meltzer, Milton. *Langston Hughes.* Brookfield, CT: Millbrook Press, 1997.

Monroe, Judy. *The Sacco and Vanzetti Controversial Murder Trial: A Headline Court Case.* Berkeley Heights, NJ: Enslow Publishers, 2000.

Munden, Kenneth W., exec. ed. *The American Film Institute Catalog of Motion Pictures Produced in the United States, Feature Films, 1921–1930.* New York, R. R. Bowker, 1971.

Nardo, Don. *The Origin of Species: Darwin's Theory of Evolution.* San Diego: Lucent Books, 2001.

Nardo, Don. *Vitamins and Minerals.* New York: Chelsea House, 1994.

O'Connell, Arthur J. *American Business in the 20th Century.* San Mateo, CA: Bluewood Books, 1999.

Orgill, Roxane. *If I Only Had a Horn: Young Louis Armstrong.* Boston: Houghton Mifflin, 1997.

Orgill, Roxane. *Shout, Sister, Shout! Ten Girl Singers Who Shaped a Century.* New York: Margaret McElderry, 2001.

Otfinoski, Steven. *Alexander Fleming: Conquering Disease With Penicillin.* New York: Facts on File, 1992.

Peacock, Judith. *Diabetes.* Mankato, MN: LifeMatters Press, 2000.

Pfleuger, Lynda. *George Eastman: Bringing Photography to the People.* Berkeley Heights, NJ: Enslow Publishers, 2002.

Pietrusza, David. *The Roaring Twenties.* San Diego: Lucent Books, 1998.

Pollard, Michael. *Margaret Mead: Bringing World Cultures Together.* Woodbridge, CT: Blackbirch Press, 1999.

Reef, Catherine. *George Gershwin: American Composer.* Greensboro, NC: Morgan Reynolds, 2000.

Riley, James A. *The Negro Leagues.* New York: Chelsea House, 1996.

Ritter, Lawrence. *The Story of Baseball.* New York: Morrow Junior Books, 1999.

Ruby, Jennifer. *Costume in Context: the 1920s and 1930s.* London: B.T. Batsford, Ltd, 1988.

Savage, Jeff. *Home Run Kings.* Austin, TX: Raintree/Steck-Vaughn, 1999.

Severance, John B. *Skyscrapers: How America Grew Up.* New York: Holiday House, 2000.

Sherrow, Victoria. *Censorship in Schools.* Springfield, NJ: Enslow Publishers, 1996.

Sherrow, Victoria. *Hardship and Hope: America and the Great Depression.* New York: Twenty-First Century Books, 1997.

Silverstein, Alvin, Virginia Silverstein, and Robert Silverstein. *Measles and Rubella.* Springfield, NJ: Enslow Publishers, 1997.

Silverstein, Alvin, Virginia Silverstein, and Robert Silverstein. *Tuberculosis.* Hillside, NJ: Enslow Publishers, 1994.

Stefoff, Rebecca. *Charles Darwin and the Evolution Revolution.* New York: Oxford University Press, 1996.

Stewart, Gail. *Diabetes.* San Diego: Lucent Books, 1999.

Stewart, Mark. *Baseball: A History of the National Pastime.* New York: Franklin Watts, 1998.

Stewart, Mark. *Football: A History of the Gridiron Game.* New York: Franklin Watts, 1998.

Tessitore, John. *F. Scott Fitzgerald: The American Dreamer.* New York: Franklin Watts, 2001.

Tessitore, John. *The Hunt and the Feast: A Life of Ernest Hemingway.* New York: Franklin Watts, 1996.

Thorn, John, Pete Palmer, and Michael Gershman, eds. *Total Baseball,* 7th ed. Kingston, NY: Total Sports, 2001.

Thorndike, Jonathan L. *The Teapot Dome Scandal Trial: A Headline Court Case.* Berkeley Heights, NJ: Enslow Publishers, 2001.

Tocci, Salvatore. *Alexander Fleming: The Man Who Discovered Penicillin.* Berkeley Heights, NJ: Enslow Publishers, 2002.

Topalian, Elyse. *Margaret Sanger.* New York: Franklin Watts, 1984.

Trespacz, Karen L. *The Trial of Gangster Al Capone: A Headline Court Case.* Berkeley Heights, NJ: Enslow Publishers, 2001.

Vaughan, William H. T. *Encyclopedia of Artists.* New York: Oxford University Press, 2000.

Wallis, Jeremy. *Coco Chanel.* Chicago: Heinemann Library, 2002.

Weitzman, David. *Model T: How Henry Ford Built a Legend.* New York: Crown Publishers, 2002.

White, G. Edward. *Oliver Wendell Holmes: Sage of the Supreme Court.* New York: Oxford University Press Children's Books, 2000.

Whitelaw, Nancy. *Margaret Sanger: Every Child a Wanted Child.* New York: Dillon Press, 1994.

Whittingham, Richard. *Rites of Autumn: The Story of College Football.* New York: Free Press, 2001.

Yancey, Diane. *Tuberculosis.* Brookfield, CT: Twenty-First Century Books, 2001.

Yannuzzi, Della A. *Ernest Hemingway: Writer and Adventurer.* Springfield, NJ: Enslow Publishers, 1998.

Yannuzzi, Della A. *Zora Neale Hurston: Southern Story Teller.* Springfield, NJ: Enslow Publishers, 1996.

Ziesk, Edra. *Margaret Mead: Anthropologist.* New York: Chelsea House, 1990.

WEB SITES

Achievements in Public Health, 1900–1999: Healthier Mothers and Babies. http://www.cdc.gov/epo/mmwr/preview/mmwrhtml/mm4838a2.htm (accessed on August 5, 2002).

The First Measured Century: Timeline Events—Stock Market Crash. http://www.pbs.org/fmc/timeline/estockmktcrash.htm (accessed on August 2, 2002).

Five Educational Philosophies: Progressivism. http://edweb.sdsu.edu/people/Lshaw/F95syll/philos/phprogr.html (accessed on August 2, 2002).

Greatest Films of the 1920s. http://www.filmsite.org/20sintro.html (accessed on August 5, 2002).

The Growth of the Federal Government in the 1920s. http://www.cato.org/pubs/journal/cj16n2-2.html (accessed on August 5, 2002).

John Dewey (1859–1952). http://www.philosophypages.com/ph/dewe.htm (accessed on August 2, 2002).

The Leaded Gas Scare of the 1920s. http://www.nrdc.org/air/transportation/hleadgas.asp (accessed on August 5, 2002).

Major Sporting Events of the 1920s. http://din-timelines.com/1920s-sport.shtml (accessed on August 5, 2002).

Media History Timeline: 1920s. http://www.mediahistory.umn.edu/time/1920s.html (accessed on August 5, 2002).

Medicine and Madison Avenue—Timeline. http://scriptorium.lib.duke.edu/mma/timeline.html#1920 (accessed on August 2, 2002).

New York Yankees History. http://newyork.yankees.mlb.com/NASApp/mlb/nyy/history/nyy_history_timeline.jsp?period=1 (accessed on August 5, 2002).

1920s. http://www.richland2.org/svh/Media/socstud/1920s.htm (accessed on August 5, 2002).

1920s. http://www.usgennet.org/usa/il/state/alhn1920.html (accessed on August 5, 2002).

The 1920s: Business and Industry Trends and Leaders of the Roaring Twenties. http://www.louisville.edu/~kprayb01/1920s-Business.html (accessed on August 2, 2002).

The 1920s: News and Politics. http://www.louisville.edu/~kprayb01/1920s-News-1.html (accessed on August 2, 2002).

1920s Oscar winners. http://www.ew.com/ew/oscar2000/history/1920.html (accessed on August 2, 2002).

Where to Learn More

The 1920s: Science, Nature, the Humanities. http://www.louisville.edu/~kprayb01/1920s-Science.html (accessed on August 2, 2002).

The 1920s: Sports and Players of the 1920s. http://www.louisville.edu/~kprayb01/1920s-Sports.html (accessed on August 2, 2002).

Sanger Fact Sheet. http://www.plannedparenthood.org/about/thisispp/sanger.html (accessed on August 5, 2002).

Scopes Trial Home Page. http://www.law.umkc.edu/faculty/projects/ftrials/scopes/scopes.htm (accessed on August 2, 2002).

TIME Person of the Year Archive—Charles Lindbergh, 1927. http://www.time.com/time/poy2000/archive/1927.html (accessed on August 5, 2002).

Index